The Story of Sonechka

Marina Tsvetaeva, one of the most acclaimed Russian twentieth-century poets and autobiographers, is well-known for the passionate and lyrical intensity of her poetry, plays, and prose. This first translation of Tsvetaeva's *The Story of Sonechka* (1936) is a welcome contribution to the ongoing project of making Tsvetaeva's œuvre available to English speakers that has been undertaken by several contemporary translators. Fishbeyn's and Reeve's admirable and praiseworthy translation of Tsvetaeva's masterpiece, written in Russian and in French, captures the spirit and the uniqueness of Tsvetaeva's mode of writing. *The Story of Sonechka* sheds light on the construction of Tsvetaeva's creative identity during the early years of the Soviet regime. Tsvetaeva's engagement with the actors from Yevgeny Vakhtangov's Third Studio of the Moscow Art Theatre inspired her early plays featuring Casanova, and developed her profound understanding of poetic theatre and commedia dell'arte that Vakhtangov used for his imaginative realism mode of artistic expression. The story is a homage to the avant-garde principles of theatricality and self-reinvention as strongly advocated by Nikolai Evreinov, whose notion of the theatricality of everyday life unlocks many semantic layers in *The Story of Sonechka*.

—*Alexandra Smith*,
Reader in Russian Studies, University of Edinburgh

With *The Story of Sonechka* C.D.C. Reeve and I.B. Fishbeyn offer an unabridged translation into English of Russian poet Marina Tsvetaeva's 1937 memoir about her brief relationship in 1918–1919 with actress Sofia Holliday. This volume includes Tsvetaeva's "story," abundantly footnoted, Reeve's introductory musings on Tsvetaeva's writing as influenced by her love affairs, and a translation of the writer's 1940 "Autobiography." In their rendering of the "story" itself, the translators valiantly took on Tsvetaeva's highly nuanced, often idiosyncratic prose, selections of her enigmatic poetry, and multiple quotations from other writers' works woven into the text. A labor of love, C.D.C. Reeve's and I.B. Fishbeyn's volume will serve specialists as well as readers new to the legacy of the renowned and tragic Russian poet.

—*Diane Nemec Ignashev*,
Class of 1941 Professor of Russian & the Liberal Arts Emeritus, Carleton College

The Story of Sonechka is a rare, warming bonfire drawn from Marina's Tsvetaeva's carefully salvaged private reserve of contemporary notebooks, wonderfully rekindled by her hand in 1937—in the poverty of her French exile. Here we find the smoke and the sparkle of a few exceptional months in Revolutionary Moscow. Told with intimacy and searing tenderness, this is Tsvetaeva's tribute to the life-changing power of youthful friendships. It is Tsvetaeva at her fiery, elegiac best—and, finally, in an admirable English translation that offers even the pleasure of reading aloud—with all Tsvetaeva's eccentric punctuation preserved. It has the power to direct your own reading voice to echo hers—in its emotional catches and firm assertions alike.

—*Mary Jane White*,
MFA Iowa, NEA Fellow in both poetry and translation

The Story of Sonechka

Marina Tsvetaeva

Translated by I. B. Fishbeyn
and C. D. C. Reeve

CHERRY ORCHARD BOOKS
2025

Library of Congress Cataloging-in-Publication Data

Names: TSvetaeva, Marina, 1892-1941, author. | Fishbeyn, I. B.
  (Inessa B.), 1962- translator. | Reeve, C. D. C., 1948- translator.
Title: The story of Sonechka / Marina Tsvetaeva ; translated by
  I. B. Fishbeyn and C. D. C. Reeve.
Other titles: Povest' o Sonechke. English (Fishbeyn, Reeve)
Description: Boston : Cherry Orchard Books, 2025. | Includes
  bibliographical references.
Identifiers: LCCN 2024053280 (print) | LCCN 2024053281 (ebook) |
  ISBN 9798887198040 (hardback) | ISBN 9798887198057 (paperback) |
  ISBN 9798887198064 (adobe pdf) | ISBN 9798887198071 (epub)
Subjects: LCSH: TSvetaeva, Marina, 1892–1941—Relations with
  Women—Fiction. | Women poets, Russian—20th century—Fiction. |
  LCGFT: Autobiographical fiction.
Classification: LCC PG3476.T75 P6813 2025 (print) | LCC PG3476.T75
  (ebook) | DDC 891.73/42—dc23/eng/20241115
LC record available at https://lccn.loc.gov/2024053280
LC ebook record available at https://lccn.loc.gov/2024053281

Copyright © 2025, C. D. C. (David) Reeve, Inessa Fishbeyn, English translation

ISBN 9798887198040 (hardback)
ISBN 9798887198057 (paperback)
ISBN 9798887198064 (adobe pdf)
ISBN 9798887198071 (epub)

Book design by Tatiana Vernikov
Cover design by Ivan Grave

Published by Cherry Orchard Books, and imprint of Academic Studies Press
1007 Chestnut St.
Newton, MA 02464, USA
press@academicstudiespress.com
www.academicstudiespress.com

For

All lovers of Marina Tsvetaeva

Contents

Acknowledgments	IX
Introduction	X
A Note on the Text	XXVI
The Story of Sonechka	1
Autobiography	159

Acknowledgments

This book was originally accepted for publication by Columbia University Press in a series funded by Read Russia, itself funded by the Russian Federation. When the latter invaded Ukraine, the press severed its connection with Read Russia and returned the rights to the book to it, which in turn assigned them to its present publisher. We are grateful to the Press and its readers, including Angela Livingstone, for their assistance, and to Professors Julie Peters (Columbia) and Stephanie Sandler (Harvard) for theirs. We are also grateful to Pierre Destrée for checking our French translations. Generous funds to support the writing and publication of the book were provided by ΔKE, the first fraternity to endow a distinguished professorship, and by the University of North Carolina at Chapel Hill.

Introduction

Marina Tsvetaeva[1] is an internationally famous poet, one of the greatest of the twentieth century, whose work has been translated into many European languages: her collected poems are available in a wonderful French edition,[2] for example, as are her collected prose works (including, *The Story of Sonechka*),[3] but—to our loss—nothing quite comparable is available in English.[4] Poetry, of course, especially poetry like Tsvetaeva's, is difficult to translate, as—for that matter—is Tsvetaeva's poetic, vivid, often extremely funny, and always autobiographical prose: "the continuation of poetry by other means," as Joseph Brodsky calls it.[5] About both, John Bayley has this to say:

---

1   Tsvetaeva's *Autobiography*, included in the present volume, gives an outline of her life and works. The best biographical study is still Simon Karlinsky, *Marina Tsvetaeva: the Woman, Her World, and Her Poetry* (Cambridge, 1985), but Lily Feiler, *Marina Tsvetaeva: The Double Beat of Heaven and Hell* (Durham, 1994) is also useful.

2   Marina Tsvetaeva, *Poésie Lyrique* (1912–1941), 2 vols., ed. and trans. Véronique Lossky (Paris, 2015).

3   Marina Tsvetaeva, *Oeuvres*, 2 vols., ed. Véronique Lossky and Tzvetan Todorov (Paris, 2009).

4   Some of her prose, with an Introduction by Susan Sontag, appears in *Marina Tsvetaeva, A Captive Spirit*, ed. and trans. J. Marin King (Woodstock, 2004), and eight of her essays on poetry can be found in *Marina Tsvetaeva: Art in the Light of Conscience* (Cambridge, MA, 1992), translated with an introduction and notes by Angela Livingstone. Some of her diaries are translated in Jamey Gambrell, *Earthly Signs: Moscow Diaries 1917–1922* (New York, 2002), and some of her letters in *Letters 1926: Boris Pasternak, Marina Tsvetaeva, Rainer Maria Rilke* (New York, 2001), with a preface by Susan Sontag. We hope ourselves to publish translations of her *Florentine Nights*—available in Italian, ed. Serena Vitale, as *Le notti fiorentine* (Rome, 2011)—as well as her untranslated autobiographical stories, "Mother's Fairytale," "Khlystovki," "Life Insurance," "Something Happened," "The Chinese Man," and "The Incident with Horses." A good place to start with Tsvetaeva's poetry is *Dark Elderberry Branch: Poems of Marina Tsvetaeva: A Reading by Ilya Kaminsky and Jean Valentine* (Farmington, 2012), which includes an audio recording of the reading.

5   Joseph Brodsky, "A Poet in Prose," in his *Less Than One: Selected Essays* (New York, 1986), 178.

The Russianness of Tsvetaeva's poetry and prose—singularly direct and forceful as they are—consists in an obvious authenticity of the emotions. Everything is felt instantly and strongly: everything is *strashny* and *vesely*—terrible and joyful—and yet about this directness there is nothing histrionic, sloppy, or self-indulgent.... The flowering of life is immensely strong, immensely spontaneous in Tsvetaeva's poetry, but that goes with an equally extraordinary precision and technical skill ... she has always been a poet's poet.... Tsvetaeva's passions, hatred of injustice, anarchy, and corruption, profound admiration for duty, honor, loyalty, and trust, are as it were the standard strong feelings, but they seem to belong to her not as a poet, even when she is writing poetry.... [Her] suicide cannot be seen as Sylvia Plath's could, as an aspect of the requirement of her art. It was simply the end of the road, a long and agonizing one.[6]

Where the poetry is concerned, to be sure, "the English, any English, tends to look like pale lemon jelly next to the megaphonic granite and barbed wire of the original."[7] But in *The Story of Sonechka* we can experience something of the truth of Bayley's description for ourselves.

As the *Story* begins, it is 1918 in Moscow. The communist revolution is in full swing. Food is scarce, living conditions harsh. Two women meet on the stage of an empty theater. One is the twenty-six-year-old poet Maria Tsvetaeva (already married to her child/husband, Sergei Efron, and the mother of two girls), the other the twenty-four-year-old actress Sonia Holliday (Sonechka). *The Story of Sonechka*, written almost twenty years later, in 1937, is the story of their love for each other. As to what sort of love it was—well, that is something of a puzzle.

Toward the end of the *Story*, in a conversation with her son Mur, Tsvetaeva says that Sonechka's "life force came from me." For, as she puts it, "if there's love—there's life; if there isn't love...." That is why, "in essence there are no characters in my story. There is love. And it acted—through persons." It is a thought that finds related expression in Iris Murdoch's deep reflections

---

6   "A Poet's Tragedy: Marina Tsvetaeva (1892–1941)," in *The Power of Delight: A Lifetime in Literature* (New York, 2005), 279–290.

7   Clarence Brown, "On Not Liking Tsvetaeva," *London Review of Books* 16, no. 17 (1994). Tsvetaeva wrote, Brown says, "like a man, and like a woman. Should I make up my mind? Impossible. She never made up her own mind, nor did she see the need. I seem to hear her scorn now for the waffling about, trying to assign her work to gender categories. The attempt is itself, in her terms, a category mistake." It's as true of the person as of her work.

on love, which she variously describes as "the perception of individuals," "the extremely difficult realization that something other than oneself is real," and "the discovery of reality." What makes that realization so difficult, is that "by opening our eyes we do not necessarily see what confronts us." And the reason we do not is that "we are anxiety-ridden animals. Our minds are continually active, fabricating an anxious, usually self-preoccupied, often falsifying veil which partially conceals the world." Love, as "the capacity to *see*," is thus what "the liberation of the soul from fantasy" consists in.[8]

The measure of love, on this way of thinking about it, lies in the quality of the vision of the beloved, the quality of the independent, spontaneous life with which she is portrayed:

> You see, my whole miracle with [Sonechka] was—that she was outside me, and not inside, not a projection of my dreams or heartsickness, but an independent thing, outside my fantasy, outside my invention, that I didn't dream up, didn't sing, that she was not in my heart—but in my room. That for just once in my whole life I hadn't added anything, but was barely a joint-owner, that is, I received—in scope and return—a full measure.

We are apt to detect, not clear-eyed vision in the phrase, "for just once in my whole life," but romantic illusions—"Eye's falsehoods," as Shakespeare calls them in *Sonnet* 137. We are apt to detect it, too, when Tsvetaeva says to Mur: "That was the name of the woman whom I, out of all women in the world, loved the most. And maybe—more than anyone. I think—more than anything. Sonechka Holliday." But the fact is that we have in *The Story of Sonechka* itself something approaching evidence for the truth of at least part of it. But that, of course, will depend on how loving—how free from fantasy—our own eyes are. "A book is a mirror," as the aphorist Georg Christoph Lichtenberg wrote;[9] what we find in it depends a lot on what we bring to it.

Tsvetaeva admits that others often did not see in Sonechka what she saw. As an actress, she had limitations:

> —Yes, very talented.... But you know she's an actress fitted only for her own roles: her own self. You see, she plays herself, meaning—she

---

8   *Existentialists and Mystics* (Harmondsworth, 1998), 215, 354, 368–369.
9   *The Waste Books* (New York, 2000), 71.

doesn't play at all. She—just lives. You see Sonechka in a room—and you've seen Sonechka on stage . . . .[10]

When she returns to Moscow from a theater tour of the provinces, but does not go to see Tsvetaeva, people spoke of her "'ungratefulness,' 'flippancy,' 'inconstancy'" and of "how unfaithful she is." But Tsvetaeva herself, confident of her own love and the clarity of vision it guarantees, did not succumb: "not for a second deep in my soul did I believe that she—for some banal reason or other—didn't come, simply didn't come—*didn't come.*"

The explanation she gives for Sonechka's not coming is this:

> Sonechka left me for her woman's destiny. Her not coming to me was only her obedience to her female lot: to love a man—in the end, it doesn't matter what kind—and to love him alone till death. In no commandment was I—my love for her, her love for me, our love—included. About her and me there wasn't any singing in the Church or writings in the Gospels. Her leaving me was a simple and honest fulfillment of the Apostle's word: "And a man shall leave his mother and father . . ." I was to her more than father and mother, without a doubt, more than that beloved man, but she had to prefer him, the unknown one. Because this is how, while creating the world, God ordained it. And, after all, we both went against "people": never against God and never against humankind.

No doubt many readers—many of us—will see not God's word at work here, but rather an ideology of heteronormativity writing itself into what is purportedly God's word. But many others, of course, will see it the way Tsvetaeva clearly does, as "woman's destiny," divinely sanctioned.

In her *Letter to the Amazon*[11]—addressed to Natalie Clifford Barney (1876–1972), an American ex-patriate, living in Paris, who "devoted her considerable fortune, her social graces and her modest writing talent to the promotion of one single cause: spiritual and physical love between

---

10   This jaundiced view of Sonechka's abilities as an actress is undermined by the many glowing critical reviews of her performances cited in Galina Brodskaya, *Sonechka Gollidei. Zhizn' e akterskaya sud'ba* [Sonechka Holliday: life and the actress's fate] (Moscow, 2003).

11   Written in French (1932–1934), and translated into English by A'Dora Phillips and Gaëlle Cogan (New York, 2016), from which we quote. Barney was nicknamed "Amazon" by her admirer, Remy de Gourmant.

women"[12]—Tsvetaeva explains in greater detail how she understands this destiny. It is a matter of "a pure and triple vital instinct—youth, perpetuation, womb":

> The end [of the relationship with the female lover] will come. The beginning of the male lover? The succession of male lovers? The stability of the husband?—The child will come.—I omit the exceptional case: the non-maternal woman.—I also omit the banal case: the young woman who is depraved, either out of instinct or fashion, the shallow pleasure lover.—I omit, as well, the lost soul, the unusual case of one who in love searches for a soul, thus—predestined to choose a woman. And the one who loves with abandon, who, in matters of love, searches for love and takes it where she will.—And the medical case.—I consider the normal case, the natural and vital case of a young woman who is wary of man and drawn toward woman and wants a child. She who, between the man (the stranger, the indifferent, or even the *revealing* enemy) and the *repressive* beloved, ends up choosing the enemy.—She prefers having a child to love.—She prefers her child to her love.[13]

Tsvetaeva is explaining why the "normal" younger woman leaves her older female lover, and is writing now almost twenty years after her relationship with Sonechka, and three years before writing her story about it. Despite that, on this point, her views seem not to have changed. Yet they seem to overlook a number of cases.

The first is the one which, from the perspective of heteronormativity, is the only truly "normal" one: that of a woman—young or old—who wants or has children and is not sexually attracted to women at all. Second, the case of a young woman who wants or has children, and is sexually attracted to women, *and to men*—the bisexual case. Third, the case of relationships between women which, while romantic and perhaps in some sense of the term erotic, are not sexual, in that they do not include activities that aim at orgasm for at least one of the partners.[14] Fourth, (to mention just one more) she leaves out otherwise "normal" cases, which break up for reasons other than "woman's fate."

---

12   Karlinsky, *Marina Tsvetaeva*, 208.
13   *Letter to the Amazon*, 12–13.
14   A criterion proposed in Rachel Elizabeth Fraser's compelling essay, "The Erotics of ASMR," *The Oxonian Review*, May 8, 2020, http://www.oxonianreview.org/wp/the-erotics-of-asmr/.

Part of what makes these four cases particularly intriguing is that they doubly include the case of Sonechka. For, as Tsvetaeva is well aware, Sonechka herself could not have children: "Marina, I'll never have children.—Why?—I don't know, the doctor told me and explained it all, but it's so complicated, all our insides . . . ." And, in point of fact, despite her relationships with men, including marriage, she never did have any.

Then there is the yet more jarring fact that Tsvetaeva's relationship with Sonechka did not include activities that aim at orgasm for at least one of the partners. Indeed, it excluded even such activities as kissing and cuddling:

> We never kissed, except when saying hello or goodbye. But I often put my arm around her shoulders, with a gesture of defense, protection, seniority. (I was three years older. In my essence, in my whole self, older. I've never had anything little in me.) I hugged her like a brother. No, it was a dry fire, pure inspiration, without an attempt to discharge, squander, realize.

It did, however, involve these things *by a sort of proxy*:

> I knew we had to separate. If I'd been a man—it would have been the most happy love—but this way—we inevitably had to separate, for her love for me would inevitably be—and was already—on the way—to loving another, who'd always be a shadow, and whom she'd always betray with me, as she inevitably did Yura and Volodya.

And since these future relationship were "fated" to involve actual sex, the relationship with Sonechka involved this too—although, again, only by proxy.

One result of this is that all of Sonechka's sexual relationships with men become in reality sexual relationships with Tsvetaeva herself, whose intervening shadow is that of the true object of love and desire. But it is equally true that their relationships with Sonechka become relationships with her:

> I'll tell you that to my joy [Volodya had] never attempted to explain his relationship with Sonechka. He knew that I knew that it was in this case—his final step *toward me*, that it was—a rapprochement, not a separation, and that in kissing her, he kissed me—kissed all three of us—himself, her, and me—we three together in the whole Spring of 1919—in her person, on her little face—kissed.

These triangles are central to *The Story of Sonechka*, in which Pavlik, Yura, and Volodya are characters almost as important as Sonechka herself. Yura's gorgeous sister Vera, indeed, was Sonechka's first schoolgirl avatar:

> I especially remember her long back with a half-untwisted plait of hair, and from the front especially her mouth, which was scornful with naturally drooping corners, and her eyes, which were the reverse of that mouth, smiling naturally, with turned-up corners. This discrepancy in her features, which resounded in me with an inexplicable excitement, … I interpreted as beauty.

Moreover, the self of the author also becomes (so to speak) split, since it is at once the female element loving another female, and the male element through whom, by proxy, she does at least some of her loving: "With Volodya, I unburdened my male soul." The bisexuality implicit in this splitting is explicit, as we shall see, in Tsvetaeva's life. Thus she herself is a case missing from her list in *Letter to the Amazon*. It seems that, taking herself as "normal," she sees female bisexuality itself to be included under that head.

With these splits and triangles, reality itself becomes resituated, life itself reconceived:

> Sonechka didn't come—because she had *already* died. Only the dead ones—don't come in that way, because they can't, because the earth is holding them. And I felt her near me for a long, long time, almost within reach of my hand, in just the same way that one feels the dead, on whose hand one can't close one's hand only because—it shouldn't be, because it would turn all the known laws upside down: equally fearing to meet the emptiness—and to meet the hand. After all, it was only from my ears and my eyes that Sonechka disappeared.

The real world is not, then, the world our senses reveal; for the ones dead in that world are alive—really alive—in that other world: the world of love. The departed—the ones who have left us—are still here, never really having left at all. In a letter of July 16, 1937, Tsvetaeva tells her Czech friend, Anna Tesková, that when she heard of Sonechka's death, she "descended into that eternal well where everything is always alive."[15]

---

15   In "Escape from Earth: A Study of Tsvetaeva's Elsewheres," *Slavic Review* 36 (1977): 644–657, a perceptive short study of Tsvetaeva's poetry, Ieva Vitins writes: "In Tsvetaeva's

It is tempting to psychologize all of this, to see it as a way of accommodating loss, as a sort of vision of eternal life. But Tsvetaeva gives us a different way to think of it. In a letter of November 17, 1940 to Tania Kvanina, a young married woman to whom she was attracted, she writes:

> The whole point is for us to love, for our heart to pound even if it should break to smithereens. I always got broken to smithereens and all of my poems are those silver smithereens of my heart.[16]

Her prose works, too, we may infer are something like these smithereens—loved things preserved: "Who remembers Sonechka now? Her hour hasn't yet struck and she lives at the bottom of a metal chest, like a not-yet-sprouted seed of her own fame, in Mama's story."[17]

If we knew no more than this story, we might also see repression at work. We might think that Tsvetaeva desired sex with Sonechka, but for one reason or another—social or personal—repressed her desire. But we do know much more. Without purporting to go into all the details, let us touch on a few of the most salient ones, as a sort of prelude.

In her autobiographical story, "My Pushkin," Tsvetaeva tells of her reaction to a scene from Tchaikovsky's *Eugene Onegin*, which her mother thinks she is too young to understand: "Like a little fool—six years old—she's fallen in love with Onegin!" But her mother is wrong: "I had fallen in love not with Onegin, but with Onegin and Tatiana (and maybe with Tatiana—a little more), with both of them jointly and—with love."[18] Infatuation, indeed, "was to remain Tsvetaeva's characteristic form of emotional contact with another person. In love, she sought romance and the acknowledgement of an intense mutual need."[19]

---

work, earth is essentially a place of exile where her persona stands 'with only one foot.' From its confines she time and again seeks to return to her original home in the sky by escaping into the worlds of dreams, poetry, and, for a while, an impassioned correspondence.... In the late twenties and thirties, by contrast, there is a conscious turning away from aerial imagery to the immediate world, and finally a turning away from poetry itself to death."

16 This and the previous letter are quoted and discussed in Karlinsky, *Marina Tsvetaeva*, 238–239. The translations are his.
17 Letter of Alya Efron (daughter of Tsvetaeva) to A. K. Tarasenkov, February 7, 1956.
18 King, *A Captive Spirit*, 336 (translation modified).
19 Karlinsky, *Marina Tsvetaeva*, 52.

Two such romances in 1910—one mild one with the poet Lev Kobylinsky and another more intense one with Vladimir Nilender—prepared her, by their failure, to fall in love with Sergey Efron, when the two met at Maximilian Voloshin's country house in Koktebel, on the eastern shore of the Black Sea. They married in Moscow in January, 1912. Their daughter Ariadna was born on September 5, 1912.[20]

So much for the prelude.

Then, in October 1914, Tsvetaeva met the openly lesbian poet Sophia (Sonia) Parnok (1885–1933),[21] who was seven years older than she, and with whom she fell instantly in love:

> The heart immediately said: "Darling!"
> I forgave you everything—at random,
> Knowing nothing—even your name!—
> O love me, o love me![22]

Their passionate and tumultuous relationship lasted until February 1916, when it was broken off—in another of those cases omitted from *Letter to the Amazon*—not by the younger woman needing to fulfill her biological destiny, but by Parnok, who had simply moved on to another lover.

Here is part of "Girlfriend 7," one of the poems Tsvetaeva wrote about their "madcap trip ... at the end of December 1914 to the ancient city of Rostov the Great, where they visited a Christmas fair and made love in a monastery hostel,"[23] while their relationship was at its most intense:

> How in the monastery hostel
> —The bell-ringing roar of sunset—
> Blissful, like birthday girls,
> We thundered, like a troop of soldiers.

---

20 The details of all of this are recounted in Feiler, *Marina Tsvetaeva*, 42–65.

21 A good study in English is Diana Burgin, *Sophia Parnok: the Life and Work of Russia's Sappho* (New York, 1994). The pioneering study is S. Poliakova, *Zakatnye oni dni: Tsvetaeva i Parnok* [The Sunset Days of Yore: Tsvetaeva and Parnok] (Ann Arbor, 1983).

22 The second stanza of "Girlfriend 9," one of the cycle of poems Tsvetaeva wrote to Parnok. Most of these are translated, with facing Russian, in Karina McCorkle, "Those Strange Moscow Ladies: Queer Identity in the Poetry of Tsvetaeva and Parnok," unpublished bachelor's thesis, UNC Chapel Hill, 2015, https://doi.org/10.17615/gp3w-mm40, 64–72, from which we quote them.

23 Karlinsky, *Marina Tsvetaeva*, 53.

> How I swore to you to get prettier
> Until old age—and spilled salt,
> How three times—you were furious!—
> I was dealt the King of Hearts.
>
> How you squeezed my head
> Fondling each curl,
> How the flower of your enamel brooch
> Chilled my lips.
>
> How I drew your narrow finger
> Across my sleepy cheek,
> How you called me a boy,
> How you liked me that way . . .

If we are to judge from these lines, the relationship was not only explicitly sexual, it was also orgasmic for both partners ("blissful . . . *we* thundered"), and cast Tsvetaeva in the boy's role (whatever exactly that might be taken to be).

Simon Karlinsky infers in addition that the affair with Sophia Parnok awakened Tsvetaeva's "sensuality and gave her the kind of erotic fulfillment that she did not get . . . from her marriage with Sergey Efron."[24] Diana Burgin[25] infers yet more, that Tsvetaeva had "apparently never experienced real passion or been capable of orgasm" before Parnok. In Parnok's own jealous poem addressed to Tsvetaeva's husband, the same claim is pretty clearly made:

> Not you, o youth, broke her spell.
> Marveling at the flame of that loving mouth
> It is not your name that will be jealous, o first one—
> *My* name will linger on the lover's lips.

But more important than the issue of primacy—especially with regard to erotic preference—is the issue of exclusivity and significance. Was Tsvetaeva orgasmic only with women, or also with men? And what sort of significance did orgasm have for her? Her relationship with Sonechka, as we saw, was sexual only by proxy and not orgasmic at all. Yet it was Sonechka "whom I, out of all women in the world, loved the most . . . more than anything."

---

24   Karlinsky, *Marina Tsvetaeva*, 52.
25   Burgin, *Sophia Parnok*, 52.

One of Tsvetaeva's letters, which may not have been accessible to these writers, provides important evidence on both these fronts. Since it is not available in English, we quote all except an irrelevant prefatory paragraph.[26] It was written to Konstantin Rodzevich, a former White Russian office, three years younger than she, and a close friend of her husband's, whom she met soon after her arrival in Prague, and who became her lover a year later. The affair lasted from September to December 1923, so the letter was written in its early days:

September 25, 1923

Dear friend,

I'm rereading about what happened last night and now make the following correction to it. A beginning with no-end (the only place where the end should be!) is never the end, but always the beginning—this is the very exact truth about my past days and years, the only key to my intense loneliness in love.

Even when one listens to music (with which love is in great accord) one waits for an end (a resolution) and if one doesn't get it, one languishes. (The whole of Scriabin is languor.) I, who am musical in my core and in my design, perhaps, more a musician than a poet, could not possibly not languish, waiting for a resolution here too. But why wasn't there even once: "wait." Oh, never, almost at the edge, one millimeter before *it*, one second, and never! Not once! It wasn't easy and not at all like that other thing I told you about[27] (it wasn't a lie, but some sort of frenzy of pride, forgive me, but it's a matter of getting used to someone), but for me to tell a stranger, for me to ask, to put myself in someone's hands so completely—no, I preferred, but there wasn't a preference: the other men were strangers, the other men had no business with me. Distrust? Pride? Shame?

All of them together. Obviously, they didn't love me very much. Obviously, I didn't love them very much. Well, maybe I loved them very much, but not in that way. Maybe they loved me very much, but were not the right ones. This is a very dim region in me, a mystery in front of which I'm standing now. And if I've never counted it as suffering,

---

26   The Russian text is in A. Saakyants and L. Mnukhin, *Marina Tsvetaeva: Pis'ma 1905–1923* (Moscow, 2012), #63–23, 687–690.

27   It isn't clear to what Tsvetaeva is referring.

that was because I, in general, thought of love as an illness, where one doesn't count the effort.

Now appreciate this following strange thing: with *the female friend*[28] I knew it all fully, why then after that was I still pulled toward men, with whom I felt incomparably less? Obviously, it was the voice of nature, a secret hope of getting it all—and incomparably more!—by some sort of miracle from a *male friend*, which I didn't believe in because it never came true! I wanted to reach it somehow without my having anything to do with it, without my knowledge, without the participation of another in whom I hadn't enough trust (give it to me! it's mine!), so I simply didn't introduce another into the circle of my (those) feelings. But there was a heartsickness, a thirst—isn't it that same heartsickness, thirst, hope that pushed me at the station toward you, back then? The longing for *complete embodiment*. Not having known the main thing—you see, I was not a full human being.

But . . . I always responded with a joke. This is something that I used to keep hidden even from myself. (In such richness—such poverty! No, let's say it didn't count, *si peu de peine et tant de plaisir*[29]—simply didn't exist!) From this came so many meetings, so many easy separations, so much easy oblivion. In the worst case scenario, I'd lost what one can carry within oneself: the soul of the other one, which I did take with me. Put simply, I didn't belong to anyone, I wasn't anybody's.

I'm writing this whole thing to you so you won't think me simpler, younger, less passionate (maybe all of these are qualities of mine?), but this is much more complex than I've let on, and maybe *more important* to me than I myself wanted to know about till today. It was a thirst, the quenching of which I didn't believe in, that's it.

And in this, with you, I'm only at the *beginning* of the road.

---

28 Obviously Parnok.
29 Tsvetaeva is recalling a story Ivan tells in Dostoevsky, *Brothers Karamazov*: "A little blonde Norman girl of twenty—a buxom, unsophisticated beauty that would make your mouth water—comes to an old priest. She bends down and whispers her sin into the grating. 'Why, my daughter, have you fallen again already?' cries the priest: 'O Sancta Maria, what do I hear! Not the same man this time, how long is this going on? Aren't you ashamed!' 'Ah, *mon père*,' answers the sinner with tears of penitence, '*Ca lui fait tant de plaisir, et à moi si peu de peine!*' [Ah, father, it gives him so much pleasure, and me so little pain!]."

> In this with you, just like in the question of me and outer life, you are the healer of my soul, because this, first of all, is the soul's illness: madness of pride or whatever you want to call it.
>
> Your business is to make me a woman and human, to finish my embodiment. It's now or never. My wager is very large.
>
> ———
>
> Now I'm re-reading this: it turns out that I don't exist. I'm remembering now this poem of 1916 (It is in *Psyche*, I'll give this book to you.)
>
> > The lights are like a thread of gold beads,
> > A taste of the night leaf on my lips.
> > Free me from the ties of the day,
> > Friends, understand, I'm of your dreams!
>
> In this was also joy.
> And remembering it, I turn the same poem to you:
>
> > Put the night ties on me!
>
> A letter just came. I'm meeting someone today. In my soul everything is over-tortured and over-twisted. A whole new sky fell on my shoulders. I look into you as into boundlessness.
>
> Love me.
>
> M.
>
> I'm asking you, please, to destroy this female document.

It's a remarkable letter, but for our purposes, it is enough to notice that it settles the issue of significance quite decisively—orgasm really was important, and not just because of the pleasure involved—along with the somewhat less important issue of primacy: Parnok was the first! And—though perhaps a bit less decisively—it also settles the issue of exclusivity.

Another letter, from September 22, cements the issue:

> You performed a miracle on me, for the first time I felt the unity of heaven and earth. Oh, I loved the earth before you appeared, and the trees! I loved it all, I was able to love it all, except for the other person, the other living being. The other person always hindered me: he was like a wall I butted up against, I couldn't do it with them. Hence

> I had a notion of myself as not a woman, but a spirit! It was not to live, but to die.[30]

To the extent, then, that erotic preference for partners of a particular gender is partly a matter of success in achieving orgasm with them, it seems clear that Tsvetaeva was erotically bisexual, able to achieve orgasm with both males and females.

These letters also help us to understand something else about Tsvetaeva, not this time about her sexual preferences, but about the terms in which she understands them. For it seems that what she takes a partner with whom she achieves orgasm to be doing is giving her soul a living body, so that without it she is not a woman, but simply a disembodied spirit. Looking back, then, at Tsvetaeva's thoughts in the *Story of Sonechka*, we might think of the life her non-orgasmic love gives to what would otherwise be just characters, not persons, as a sort of spiritual life.

The brief affair with Rodzevich was in 1923. By 1937, Tsvetaeva had had a son (February 1, 1925) and many more affairs with men and women, none lasting, none satisfying.[31] Moreover, Tsvetaeva's life didn't end in 1937: with her daughter Irina, long dead of starvation in a children's shelter (February 2, 1920), her other daughter, Alya, imprisoned in a labor camp (she was arrested on August 27, 1939), her husband Sergei in prison (he was shot there on October 16, 1941), at odds with her son Mur, driven mad by Stalin's apparatus of terror—she died by her own hand on August 31, 1941.[32] What, we must now wonder again, therefore, is what was so special about

---

30   Feiler, who quotes this letter, differently translated, concludes that with Rodzevich, Tsvetaeva "seemed to experience something of the same intensely sexual feelings for him as she had for Parnok" (Feiler, *Marina Tsvetaeva*, 145). The text we translate is in Saakyants and Mnukhin, *Marina Tsvetaeva*, 62–23, 682.

31   They are recounted chronologically in Feiler, *Marina Tsvetaeva*. There were also some apparent attempts at some sort of relationship in 1940 with the young woman we encountered earlier, Tania Kvanina. McCorkle ("Those Strange Moscow Ladies," 17–21) provides some details of this relationship, supported by quotations from Kvanina's memoirs. These record Tsvetaeva as having told her that she "greatly resembled Sonechka, only a grown-up Sonechka" (19). But McCorkle is a bit too quick to see sexual attraction, rather than nostalgic re-enactment of a relationship not straightforwardly sexual, as Tsvetaeva's motivation.

32   The fullest account is Irma Kudrova, *The Death of a Poet: The Last Days of Marina Tsvetaeva* (Woodstock, 2004).

the relationship with Sonechka, that it—more even than any of the straightforwardly sexual and orgasmic ones—made her "the woman whom I, out of all women in the world, loved the most. And maybe—more than anyone. I think—more than anything"? If the answer lies anywhere, it must lie in the *Story of Sonechka* itself, we suggest, and the quality of the picture of her that it presents.

One part of Tsvetaeva's answer has to do with the sense she has of the declining powers of her own love, and her need to conserve what she has left of them:

> Do I need to add that after her I never loved another female creature and, of course, won't love any, because I love less and less, saving the rest of my left-over ardor for those—who won't be able to feel its warmth?

But when we ask for whom she must conserve them, the only plausible answer, it seems, the only ones "who won't be able to feel its warmth" are those—of whom Sonechka is the principal example—who have passed out of reach of "eyes and ears." So that doesn't really help much, since it just returns us to the question of Sonechka's specialness. An earlier passage is more illuminating:

> Here it's appropriate to say, because later it will be obvious, that I also treated Sonechka as one would a favorite thing, a present, with a feeling of happy possession one never felt before or after—for a person, but for favorite things—always. Not even for a favorite book, but precisely—for a ring, which finally managed to get on the requisite hand, something screamingly—mine, still on the burial mound—mine, in the possession of that gypsy—mine, a ring as happy to be mine as I—to have it, fitting me, as I intrinsically, inalienably—fit it. If anything—at one with my finger! Our relationship wasn't exhausted by this: it was all my conceivable love plus *this*.

This fittingness and harmony—palpable in the *Story*—explains why being with the living, breathing Sonechka was so joyfully pleasant. But what it doesn't explain is the continuation of the relationship—to put it this way—with a Sonechka who is no longer there to continue the harmonious duet (or trio!).

Fortunately, then, Tsvetaeva's attempts to explain Sonechka's specialness don't stop there:

> Like Cordelia about—salt—from my children's book of Shakespeare's *King Lear*, the same am I about—Sonechka and sugar, with the same modesty: she was necessary for me—like sugar. As everyone knows—sugar—is not a necessity, one can live without it, and for four years of the Revolution, we did live without it, some substituting—treacle—for it, some—shredded beets, some—saccharin, some—nothing at all. Drinking unsweetened tea. No one dies of its absence. But they don't live either. Without salt, scurvy happens, without sugar, heartsickness. A *whole* live, white, piece of sugar—that's what Sonechka was for me. Crude? Crude—like Cordelia: "I love according to my salt,[33] no more, no less." One can love the old King like salt... but a little girl? No, enough of salt. Let this be said once in the world, I loved her like sugar during revolution. And that's that.

We are hardly in a position to doubt her: "the art of our necessities is strange," and heartsickness-dispelling sugar in Moscow in 1919 was surely no small thing. Like a happy childhood, even the memory of it continues to work its energizing magic, especially on an increasingly tragic life: "I dream about Sonechka Holliday, like about a lump of sugar: a *guaranteed*—sweetness." Tsvetaeva's wish, indeed, was that the *Story of Sonechka* might serve its readers in precisely that role: "Let this whole story be—like a lump of sugar, at least it was *sweet* to write it!"

---

33 *Sol!* as in salary, translates "bond."

A Note on the Text

Part I of *The Story of Sonechka*, was first published in *Russkiye Zapiski* 3 (Paris, Shanghai, 1938); part II was first published in *Neizdannoe, stikhi, teatr, proza* (Paris, 1976). A censored version of the entire work was first published in *Novy mir* (Moscow, 1979). The text translated is that printed in A. Saakyants and L. Mnukhin, *Marina Tsvetaeva, Sobraniye Sochinyenei v Syeme Tomakh*, Tom 4 (Moscow, 1994), 293–418.

Tsvetaeva's idiosyncratic punctuation is an intrinsic part of her prose style, which it is important to preserve in translation.

The Story of Sonechka

Thank you for Sonechka. Mama loved her very much. . . . Who remembers Sonechka now? Her hour hasn't yet struck and she lives at the bottom of a metal chest, like a not-yet-sprouted seed of her own fame, in Mama's story. On one beautiful day they will both be resurrected—Mama and Sonechka, hand in hand. And everyone will love them again. That real, post-death love, called public recognition, doesn't come soon, but it's much more solid and unalterable than any occurring during one's lifetime.

—Letter of Alya Efron to A. K. Tarasenkov,
February 7, 1956

I

Pavlik and Yura

> She was pale—but somehow rosy pink,
> A little one—with lots of splendid hair
>
> —Victor Hugo[1]

No, there wasn't any paleness in her, not in anything of hers, everything in her was the opposite of paleness, but nonetheless she was "somehow rosy pink," which is going to be shown and proven in due course.

It was the winter of 1918–19, and it is now still winter 1918, December. I gave a reading of my play, *Snowstorm*, to the students of Studio Number Three, in some theater or other, on a stage. An empty theater, a full stage.

Snowstorm was dedicated to Yura and Vera Z.,[2] to their friendship, with my love. Yura and Vera were brother and sister. Vera was my schoolmate in the last year of high school, but not a classmate. I was a year older and saw her only during recess: a skinny, curly haired, girlish puppy. And I especially remember her long back with a half-untwisted plait of hair, and from the front especially her mouth, which was scornful with naturally drooping corners, and her eyes, which were the reverse of that mouth, smiling naturally, with turned-up corners. This discrepancy in her features, which resounded in me with an inexplicable excitement, and which I interpreted as beauty, seemed surprising to others, who found nothing like beauty in her, and that, in its turn, surprised me. I'll tell you right away that I was correct, and that she later turned out to be

---

[1]   *Elle était pale–et pourtant rose,*
          Petite–avec de grands cheveux...
    From Victor Hugo (1802–1885), French poet, novelist, and dramatist. Tsvetaeva quotes from an untitled poem in his *Contemplations* (1856).

[2]   Yury Alexandrovich Zavadsky (Yura Z., Yury Z., Z-sky) (1894–1977), actor, director, and his sister Vera Alexandrovna Zavadskaya (1895–1930).

a beauty, and so much of a beauty that in 1927, in Paris, when she was gravely sick, on her last legs, they tried to put her on the big screen.

With this Vera, to this Vera, I've never spoken a word, and now, nine years after school, while dedicating *Snowstorm* to her, I thought with fear that she wouldn't understand a thing in it, because perhaps she doesn't remember me and maybe she never noticed me at all.

(But why Vera, when this is about Sonechka? Well, Vera is the root, the pre-story, the most ancient beginning of Sonechka, which is a very short story with a very long pre-story. And after-story.)

How did Sonechka start? How did she come alive in my life?

It was October 1917. Yes, that very October. That very last October day, that is, the first day of the Moscow Bolshevik Uprising's[3] end (the borders were rumbling still). I rode in a dark train car from Moscow to the Crimea. Above my head, on the top bunk, a young man's voice was loudly reciting poetry. As follows:

> And here it is, the dream of the grandfathers,
> Who drank the cognac and had the great discuss,
> In Girondins'[4] cloaks, through snow and troubles,
> With downcast bayonets burst in on us.
>
> And ghosts of guardsmen, Decembrists,
> Over snow the Pushkin Neva way,
> Led regiments to the buglers' calls,
> And military music's loudest wail.
>
> The Emperor[5] in bronze boots called thee,
> The Preobrazhensky Regiment,[6]
> When in the gulfs of streets prostrate,
> Was silenced the dashing clarinet.

---

3   October 25—November 2, 1917.

4   The Girondins or Girondists were members of a loosely knit monarchist political faction during the French Revolution.

5   Peter the Great (1672–1725). The poem echoes Pushkin's narrative poem, "The Bronze Horsman."

6   One of the oldest most elite regiments in the imperial Russian Army, formed by Peter the Great.

> The Miracle Worker recollected,
> Hearing the Petropavlovsky[7] cannonade,
> That mad reluctant voice's sound,
> That memorable sound: "Just wait!"

What is that, tell me at once who wrote it?—The author is seventeen; he's still in school. He's a comrade of mine—Pavlik A.[8]

The cadet is proud because his friend is a poet. A *military* cadet, who had been fighting for five days, compensating himself with poems for his defeat. The spirit of Pushkin wafted through the air. It was *that* kind of friendship. And his response from the bunk above: He looks very much like Pushkin. Small, brisk, with curly hair and side-whiskers, even the boys in Pushkino village call him Pushkin. He's always writing. Every morning a new poem:

> Infanta, know this! I'm ready to burn at any stake
> As long as I know your eyes will gaze on me.

It's from his play, *The Doll-Infanta*. It's what the Dwarf tells the Infanta. He loves her. The Dwarf is Pavlik A. himself. True, he's really small, but not at all a dwarf.

> ... One alone—under so many names ...[9]

The first, the very first, thing I did when I returned from the Crimea was to find this Pavlik. He lived somewhere near the Cathedral of Christ the Savior[10] and I, somehow, entered his house through the back door, and so our meeting took place in the kitchen. Pavlik was in his school uniform with buttons, which

---

7   The Peter and Paul Cathedral, a Russian Orthodox cathedral inside the Peter and Paul Fortress in St. Petersburg.

8   Pavel Grigorevich Antokolsky (1896–1978), a poet and actor belonging to the Second Studio.

9   From Aeschylus, Prometheus Bound.

10 The Cathedral of Christ the Savior, a Russian Orthodox cathedral in Moscow, a few hundred meters southwest of the Kremlin.

emphasized even more his resemblance to Pushkin-as-student-at-the-Lyceum, the young Pushkin, only—the black-eyed one: the Pushkin—of legend.[11]

Neither he nor I was embarrassed by the kitchen, something pushed us toward each other, through all the little saucepans and pots—so that we inner-rattled ourselves, no less than those vats and pots did. Our meeting was like an earthquake. By the same token that I realized who he was, he realized who I was. (I'm not talking about poems, I didn't even know if he knew my poems.)

After standing in a magic stupor, for who knows how long, we went out by the same back door, overflowing with poems and talk...

In short, Pavlik went and disappeared. Disappeared for a long time into my Borisoglebsky Lane place. He sat for days, he sat for mornings, he sat for nights... As an example of his sitting I'll give you just one of our dialogs:

I (*timidly*):

—Pavlik, do you think that what we're doing now could be called thinking?

Pavlik (*even more timidly*):

—It's called sitting on the clouds and governing the world.

Pavlik had a friend about whom he was always talking: Yura Z.[12]—"Yura and I... When I read this to Yura... Yura's always asking me... Yesterday, Yura and I purposely and loudly kissed, so everyone would think that he, finally, had fallen in love... And only think: the student-actors all jumped out, and there, instead of a maiden—was I!!!"

In one beautiful evening he brought this "Yura" to me.—"And this, Marina, is my friend, Yura Z."—with equal force on each word, overflowing each equally.

Raising my eyes, which took a long time, since Yura went on and on and on, I found *Vera's* eyes and mouth.

—Dear God, you aren't a brother of... Of course, you are her brother... You cannot not have a sister named Vera!

---

11 Even though there are many portraits of Pushkin, it is difficult to determine the true color of his eyes. Since he is of African descent many thought that his eyes are black, but on the so-called "ticket to Saint-Petersburg" (December 28, 1825), he says that "the hair is dark-blond, the eyes are blue, the beard shaved off."

12 "Yura" is the familiar form.

—She is the one he loves most in the world!

Yura and I started talking. We talked, Yura and I, while Pavlik was silent and silently was swallowing us—together and separately—with his huge heavy hot eyes.

In the same evening, which was—a deep dark night, which became—a very early morning, after parting with them under my poplar trees, I wrote a poem for them together:

> Sleep with un-parted arms and hands,
> Brother with brother, friend with friend,
> Together in the self-same bed...
> Together sang, together drank...
>
> I wrapped them up in plaid,
> Falling forever into love,
> Through eyes closed over,
> Strange news I read:
> Rainbow: double fame,
> Glow: double death.
>
> Their arms I'll not un-part!
> I'd rather, rather I'll,
> Embrace a flame of hell.[13]

But instead of a flame, *Snowstorm*. So, to keep my word—to not un-part *their* arms, I had to unite in my own love—the other hands: those of brother and sister. Or in yet simpler terms: I had not to love Yura *alone* and by that deprive Pavlik, with whom I could only "rule the world." I needed to love Yura plus something else. But the something else couldn't be Pavlik, because Yura plus Pavlik was already a given—I had to love Yura plus Vera. This somehow scattered him around, but in reality—strengthened and concentrated him, because everything not in the brother was found in the sister, and everything not in the sister was in the brother. A terribly, intolerably full love fell to my lot. (The fact that Vera was sick in the Crimea and didn't know about it didn't change anything.)

The relationship from the beginning—had a condition. A silently agreed to and established condition: that they'd always come together—and leave

---

13 "Brothers" (1918).

together. But since no relationship can be conditional from the beginning, one lovely morning, the telephone rang:

—Is that you?

—It is.

—Can I not come sometimes without Pavlik?

—Like when?

—Today.

(But where is Sonechka? Sonechka is already nearby, almost behind the door, though in time—one more year.)

However, this crime was punished immediately: tête-à-tête, Yura Z. and I were simply bored, since about the main thing, that is, about me and him, him and me, us, we couldn't bring ourselves to speak. We behaved ourselves better without him than in front of Pavlik! But as for the rest—it wasn't successful.

He fiddled with some little things on my desk, he asked about portraits, and I—didn't even dare to talk about Vera, so much of Vera was—him. So, we sat, incubating who knows what, hatching the sole moment of goodbye, when I, seeing him out through the back entrance down the spiral staircase, stopped on the last step, where he was still a head taller than I—and nothing, just glaces:

—Yes?

—No.

—But maybe yes.

—For now, not yet.

And a double smile: his of rapturous admiration and mine of uneasy triumph. (One more victory like this—and we're defeated.) This lasted a year.

I didn't get to read *Snowstorm* to him in January of 1918. Only someone with a rich life could be given that present, and since he, during our long sittings, didn't seem to have one, and Pavlik—did, I presented it to Pavlik—as a grateful revenge for his *Infanta*, which was also not dedicated to me. For Yura, biding my time, I picked the most difficult thing (and for me—an impoverished one), namely, reading my poem to him in front of the whole Third Studio (all were—students of Vakhtangov,[14] Yura, Pavlik and the other one, in the dark car of the train, who read "Freedom,"[15] and then was immediately

---

14 Yevgeny Bagartionovich Vakhtangov (1883–1922), a Russian actor and theater director who founded the Vakhtangov Theater.

15 Tsvetaeva is referring to the poem of Pavlik A.; "Freedom" isn't its official title.

killed in the Army) and mainly in front of Vakhtangov himself, their God and Father—their Commander.

After all, my goal was to give him as much as possible, and as much as possible—for an actor—is when there are more people, more ears, more eyes...

And now, more than a year after our first meeting with our hero, and a year after I completed *Snowstorm*—there was that very stage, full of people, and an empty hall.

(My precision is boring, I know. The reader is indifferent to the dates and I damage the artistry of the thing with them. But for me they are vital and even holy. For me every year, and even each season of those years, appears—with a face: 1917, Pavlik A.; winter 1918, Yura Z; spring 1919, Sonechka... I simply cannot see her outside of this 9, this double 1 and double 9, alternating 1's and 9's. My exactness is—my last, post-mortal loyalty.)

So—this very full stage and empty hall. Brightly lit stage and black hall.

From the first second of reading my face started burning—so much so, that I was afraid—my hair would catch fire, I even felt the fine crackles like a fire before its peak.

I was reading—I may tell you—in a *scarlet* fog, not seeing my notebook, not seeing the lines, I read from memory, on the off chance that it would turn out okay, in one gulp—like drinking!—but also like singing!—in my most melodious, heart-rending voice:

> ...And in the desert of the count's rooms will float
> The high moon.
> You, woman, don't remember anything,
> You don't remember... (*Persistently.*)
> You shouldn't...
> For the she-wanderer—sleep.
> For the he-wanderer—a road.
> Remember!—Forget.
> (*She's asleep. From the windows come the sound of irrevocably vanishing bells.*)

When I finished—everyone started talking immediately. They talked as *fully* as I—fell silent.—Splendid.—Extraordinary.—Genius.—Theatrical.—And so on.—Yura will be playing the Gentleman.—And Lila S.[16] the old lady.—And

---

16   Elena Vladimirovna Shik (1895–1931), an actress, theater director, and teacher.

Yura S. the merchant.—And the music, those very irrevocable bells—Yura N. will write. But there's a problem—who is to play the Lady in the cloak?

And then the least ceremonious remark, right here, in front of everyone:—*You* can't.—Your bust's too large. (*Another version:* legs too short.) (*I, silently:* The Lady in the cloak is—my soul. Nobody can play it.)

Everyone was talking and I was burning. After they finished talking—they started over-thanking me.—For a great pleasure... For such rare happiness... All strange faces—strangers. A fat lot of good. Finally—he: the Gentleman in the cloak. He didn't come up to me, but moved off, separating me from the rest, and separating himself and me with his height, like a cloak, at the edge of the stage:—"Verochka[17] is the only one who is capable of playing the Lady in the cloak. She is the one to play her." *To their friendship, with my love?*

—And this, Marina (*in a low ceremonious Pavlik voice*) is—Sophia Evgenevna Holliday. Said in exactly the same way as a year ago: And this, Marina, is—my friend, Yura Z. But in place of *my friend*—something—was swallowed up. (In this same moment I feel at my shoulder Yura Z. moving away.)

In front of me stands—a little girl. I *know* this is Pavlik's Infanta! With two black braids, two huge black eyes, and blazing cheeks.

In front of me is—a live fire. Everything is burning, the whole of her—burning! Her cheeks are burning, her lips are burning, her eyes are burning, in the fire of her mouth burn her fireproof white teeth. Her braids—as if curling from a flame—are burning! Two black braids, one on the back and the other on her breast, as if the first one was thrown off by the fire. And the glance from this flame was—of such admiration, such despair: such I fear! such: I love!

—Does it really happen? Such taverns... snowstorms... loves? Such Gentlemen in cloaks that come especially, so as to leave forever? I always knew it—*did* know it, now I *do* know—it does. Because it—truly—happened: You really were standing there. Because it was *you* standing. And the old lady—sat. And she knew it all. And the Snowstorm wailed. And the Snowstorm swept him up to the door. And then—swept him aside... swept the tracks away... And what happened when she woke up the next morning? The next morning she didn't wake up. The next morning they found her in a field. Oh, why didn't he take her with him in the sleigh? Why didn't he take her in his fur coat?

---

17   Tsvetaeva may be thinking of Vera Z., to whom Snowstorm is dedicated.

—She mumbles as if she's asleep. With open—as wide as they could open—eyes! She's sleeping, sleeping in reality. As if we are alone with her, as if nobody's around, and I'm—not there. And when I, somehow released, finally, turn around—there really wasn't anyone on stage. They felt it, or maybe just taking the opportunity, noiselessly, soundlessly walked out. The stage was—ours.

And only then did I notice that I was still holding her little hand in mine.

———

—Oh. Marina! How scared I got! And I cried afterward... When I saw you, heard you, I fell in love right away, so madly I fell in love. I understood that it's impossible not to love you madly—and that I myself fell in love with you in that way immediately.

—But he *did not*.

—Yes, and now it's over. I don't love him anymore. I love you. And I despise him because he doesn't love you—on his knees.

—Sonechka! Did you notice then that my face was burning?

—Burning? No. I even thought, what a tender blush...

—Well then, I was burning inside me, and I was afraid—I'd burn the whole stage—the whole theater, the whole of Moscow. I thought it was—because of him, for him, *that* him, to whom—I myself—read—in front of everyone for the first time. But then I understood: my burning was for you, Sonechka... There was no me, no you. But a love still emerged. Ours.

This was my last blush, in December 1918. The whole of Sonechka was—my last blush. Roughly from that time I turned this color—no color. My face did, which it's very unlikely I'll separate from—till my last no color.

Burning for her? Or just a reflection of her short permanent fire?

...I'm happy that my last blush fell on Sonechka.

———

—Sonechka, where—with your mad life did this blush of yours come from? You don't sleep, don't eat, cry, love.

—Oh, Marina! You see—it's from my last strength!

———

That's the justification for the first part of my epigraph:

She was pale... but somehow rosy pink.[18]

That is—from this whole misfortune—she was supposed to be pale, but collecting her last strength—and saying no!—she burned. Sonechka's blush was a hero's blush. The blush of a person who decided to burn and to warm. I often saw her in the mornings, after a sleepless night with me, in that early, early hour, after our late, late conversation, when all faces—even the youngest ones—are the color of the green sky in the window, the color of sunrise. But no! Sonechka's small, dark-eyed face burned, like a non-extinguished rosy pink lantern in a port street. Yes, of course, it was—a port and she—a lantern, and all of us were that poor, poor sailor for whom it was time to get back to his ship, to wash the deck and devour the wave...

Sonechka, I'm at Lacanau-Océan,[19] portraying you. (Oh, if only it could be: "I'm at Lacanau-Océan, writing to you," but no it can't.) I'm at Lacanau-Océan, where you've never been and never will be, portraying you. On its edges and mainly on its islands, there are many black eyes. The sailors know.

She had laughter so close to tears and tears so close to laughter, though I do not remember seeing them flow. One might say: her eyes were too hot to let them flow, that they dried as soon as they appeared. It was for this reason that these beautiful eyes, always ready to weep, were not damp eyes. On the contrary, they were eyes which, while shining with tears, gave warmth, gave the image, the sensation of warmth, and not of moisture, since with all their goodwill, and the bad will of others, they succeeded in not letting one tear flow.

Yet somehow... yes!

They were beautiful, beautiful, like seedless raisins, and I swear to you that they were burning, and that seeing her cry one laughed with pleasure! Perhaps this is what we call "crying hot tears"? So, I saw a human being who has really hot tears. All the others, mine, like those of other people, are cold or lukewarm, hers were burning, and the fire of her cheeks was so powerful that

---

18 See note 1.
19 In Southwest France.

one could see them as falling—rose petals. Hot as blood, as round as pearls, salty as the sea.

. . . One could say that she was crying Mozart.[20]

And here is what Edmond About says about Sonechka's eyes in his wondrous *The King of the Mountains*[21]:

> What eyes she had, my dear Sir! I hope, for your peace of mind, that you will never meet their like. They were neither blue nor black, but of a color especially and uniquely their own. It was an ardent and velvety brown, which one sees only in Siberian garnets, and in certain garden flowers. I could show you a certain scabiosa, and a variety of hollyhock, nearly black, which recall, without capturing, the marvelous nuance of her eyes. If you have ever visited a forge at midnight, you have doubtless remarked the strange color, which gleams from a red-hot steel plate, as it changes to a reddish brown. That too was like her eyes . . . One read in them, as in a book, the whole wisdom of women and the innocence of children. But it would have blinded one to read the book for long. Her glance burned, as truly as my name is Hermann. It would have ripened the peaches on your garden wall.[22]

---

20 Perhaps a quotation from an unknown source:
   Elle avait le rire si près des larmes et les larmes si près du rire—quoique je ne me souvienne pas de les avoir vues couler. On aurait dit que ses yeux étaient trop chauds pour les laisser couler, qu'ils les séchaient lors même de leur apparition. C'est pour cela que ces beaux yeux, toujours prêts à pleurer, n'étaient pas des yeux humides, au contraire—des yeux qui, tout en brillant de larmes, donnaient chaud, donnaient l'image, la sensation de la chaleur—et non de l'humidité, puisqu' avec toute sa bonne volonté—mauvaise volonté des autres—elle ne parvenait pas à en laisser couler une seule.
   Et pourtant—si!
   Belles, belles, telles des raisins égrénés, et je vous jure qu'elles étaient brûlantes, et qu'en la voyant pleurer—on riait de plaisir! C'est peut-être cela qu'on appelle «pleurer à chaudes larmes?» Alors j'en ai vu, moi, une humaine qui les avait vraiment chaudes. Toutes les autres, les miennes, comme celles des autres, sont froides ou tièdes, les siennes étaient brûlantes, et tant le feu de ses joues était puissant qu'on les voyait tomber—roses. Chaudes comme le sang, rondes comme les perles, salées comme la mer.
   . . . On aurait dit qu'elle pleurait du Mozart.

21 A novel published in 1857. Edmond François Valentin About (1828–1885) was a French novelist, publicist, and journalist.

22 *—Quels yeux elle avait, mon cher Monsieur! Je souhaite pour votre repos que vous n'en rencontriez jamais de pareils. Ils n'etaient ni bleus ni noirs, mais d'une couleur spéciale et personnelle faite exprès pour eux. C'etait un brun ardent et velouté qui ne se rencontre que dans le grenat de Sibérie et dans certaines fleurs des jardins. Je vous montrerai une scabieuse et une variéte de rose tremière presque noire qui rappellent, sans la rendre, la nuance merveilleuse de*

Do you understand Pavlik's exclamation now?

> Infanta, know! I'm ready to burn at any stake
> As long as I know your eyes will gaze on me.

My description is a modest one: Brown eyes, the color of a horse chestnut, with something gold on the bottom, dark-brown with—amber—on the bottom: not Baltic: Eastern: the red one. Almost black with—red gold—on the bottom, which from time to time rose up to the surface: the amber—melted: the eyes with—sunken to the bottom—melted amber.

And one more thing: her eyes were slightly squinty: there were too many lashes and it seemed that—they hindered seeing: they hindered us from seeing them, the eyes, as little as its rays hinder us from seeing a star. And one more thing: even when they cried—these eyes laughed. And that is why nobody believed in their tears. Moscow doesn't believe in tears.[23] *That* Moscow—didn't believe in—*these* tears. I alone believed in them.

In general, they didn't trust her. About her, in general, in response to my effusive raptures, they responded ... with restraint ... and even this restraint was—out of respect for me, holding back their overt judgment and condemnation.

—Yes, very talented ... But you know she's an actress fitted only for her own roles: her own self. You see, she plays herself, meaning—she doesn't play at all. She—just lives. You see Sonechka in a room—and you've seen Sonechka on stage ...

Sonechka on stage:

She comes out—a little thing, in a white dress, with two black braids, lays her hands on the back of the chair and tells us:

—I lived with Babushka ... We rented a little apartment ... There was a tenant ... books ... Babushka pinned me to her dress ... And I was ashamed ...

---

ses yeux. Si vous avez jamais visité les forges à minuit, vous avez du remarquer la lueur étrange que projette une plaque d'acier chauffée au rouge brun: voilà tout justement la couleur de ses regards. Toute la science de la femme et toute l'innocence de l'enfant s'y lisaient comme dans un livre; mais ce livre, on serait devenu aveugle à le lire longtemps. Son regard brûlait, aussi vrai que je m'appelle Hermann. Il aurait fait mûrir les pêches de votre espalier.

23 A Russian proverb meaning that tears can't wash away or justify wrongdoing and will not arouse sympathy.

It was *her* life, *her* Babushka, *her* childhood, *her* "silliness" . . . *her* White Nights.²⁴

The whole city knew Sonechka. It was Sonechka—they went to see. It was for Sonechka—they went—"Did you see her? The little one in the white dress with the braids . . . Well, adorable!" Nobody knew her name, they called her: "the little one" . . .

White Nights was an event.

The performance was complex, tripartite.²⁵ First: Turgenev's, "A Story of Lieutenant Yergunov": about a young she-devil, a deceiver, somewhere in a suburban slum, fooling around, bewitching a young lieutenant. After all the promises and all the seductions, she vanished—like smoke. With his wallet. I remember how at the beginning she's waiting for him, sprucing—herself and her place up. In the middle of a huge barn—a shoe. Lonely and worn out. And here—with a kick of her leg—it flies across the whole stage. The sprucing-up is finished!

But this is—not Sonechka. This is only an introduction—to Sonechka.

Second part? It seems to me it was—something marine, something port-like, sailor-like—maybe, Maupassant: a brother and sister? It has disappeared.

And the third part. The curtains open: a chair. And behind the chair, holding onto its back—Sonechka. And here she tells us, timidly, smilingly about Babushka, about the tenant, about their poor life, about her maidenly love. In the same manner, timidly smiling and with gleaming eyes and tears as at my place in Borisoglebsky Lane, telling me about Yurochka²⁶—or about Eugene Bagartionovich—in the same way, not playing a role, or so seriously playing it, as to the death, and most of all playing—with the ends of her braids (which, by the way, were never tied with ribbons, but self-tied, self-twined naturally), or with the locks of hair on her temples, moving them away from her eyelashes,

---

24   A novella by F. M. Dostoevsky (1821–1881).

25   The performance was called "The Journals of the Studio," and was in three parts: Part 1 consisted of Chapters V–VIII of the novel *No Way Out* by N. S. Leskov (1831–1895); Part 2 of scenes from *Lieutenant Yergunov's Story* by I. S. Turgenev (1818–1883); Part 3 of "Nasten'ka's Story," night number two of Dostoevsky's *White Nights*. As for Maupassant (1850–1893), whom Tsvetaeva mentions, his work was part of another Studio's three-part performance: Part 1 consisted of *In the Port* by Maupassant; Part 2 of *A Torture Garden* by Octave Mirbeau (1848–1917); Part 3 of *The Rising of the Moon* by Lady Gregory (1852–1932), in which Sonechka may not have appeared.

26   Another familiar form of Yury.

and entertaining her hands this way when they became tired of the chair. So, the ends of her braids and the locks on her temples are—the whole of Sonechka's *play*.

I think even the dress on her wasn't theatrical, a make-believe one, but her own summer dress—from her sixteenth year maybe?

—I went to see a performance at Second Studio and saw your Sonechka...

That's how she became right away for everyone, my Sonechka—in the same way *mine* as my silver rings or bracelets—or my apron decorated with coins—something no one ever thought of disputing—since no one but me had need of it.

Here it's appropriate to say, because later it will be obvious, that I also treated Sonechka as one would a favorite thing, a present, with a feeling of happy possession one never felt before or after—for a person, but for favorite things—always. Not even for a favorite book, but precisely—for a ring, which finally managed to get on the requisite hand, something screamingly—mine, still on the burial mound—mine, in the possession of that gypsy—mine, a ring as happy to be mine as I—to have it, fitting me, as I intrinsically, inalienably—fit it. If anything—at one with my finger! Our relationship wasn't exhausted by this: it was all my conceivable love plus *this*.

One more thing: Somehow, I was insulted, irritated, and wounded when she was called Sofia Evgenevna (as if she was an adult!), or simply Holliday (as if she was a man!), or even Sonya—as if people weren't generous enough to say Sonechka! In this I saw indifference, I saw soullessness. I saw even unintelligence. Don't they (male and female) understand that she—is exactly Sonechka, and that to call her anything else—is rudeness, that about her one shouldn't talk—*without* endearment. Because Pavlik called her Holliday (he started with Infanta!), I became colder to him. For not only in the case of Sonechka, but to call any women in her absence (unless she's some sort of public figure) by her last name is—familiarity, an abuse of absence and a lowering of her, a turning of her into a man. But to call her behind her back—by a child's name—is a sign of closeness and affection, and cannot wound motherly feeling—not even an empress's. (Isn't it funny? I was only two or three years older than Sonechka, but I was insulted on her behalf—like a mother.)

No, all who loved me: read it in me and called her Sonechka—to me. With the respectful addition of—"your."

But as for now she still stands in front of us, holding onto the back of the chair. Let's emphasize her appearance—to avoid any misunderstanding: On the surface she, with her eyelashes and braids, with all her red and brown colors, could seem a Ukrainian, a Small-Russian. But—only on a superficial glance: there was nothing typical or national in this little face. It was very delicate, the work of her face: the work—of a master. I'll say one more thing: In this face was something shell-like—the way the ocean works it—something of the shell's curl, a bend of the nostrils, a curve of the lips, a general curl of the eyelashes—and little ear! Everything was fretted, chiseled, and at the same time flowing, as if this thing was *worked* and *played with*. It was not only the Ocean's work, but also the play of the waves. "I have never seen rose-pink pearls, but I'm insisting that her face was a pearlier and a yet rosier pink."[27]

How did she come to me? When? In the winter she wasn't in my life. So—it was in the spring. In the spring of 1919. And not in the earliest part of the spring, but—the April spring, I suppose, because I connect the feathered poplar trees in front of my house with her. In the season of the first tiny green leaves.

My first vision of her at my place was—on the couch, cross-legged, no light in my room, yet with sunrise in the window. And her first words in my ears were—a complaint:

—How I was afraid of you then! How afraid I was that you'd take him away from me! Because not to love—you, Marina, not to fall in love with you—on one's knees—was unthinkable, inconceivable, and simply (*with surprised eyes*)—silly? That's why I didn't for so long come to *you*, because I *knew* that I'd love you so, you, whom he loves, because of whom he *doesn't* love me. I didn't know what to do with this love of mine, because I *already* loved you, from the first moment on stage, when you had just cast your eyes down—to read. And then—what a knife in my heart! what a knife!—when he came to you *last* and you stood with him on the edge of the stage, fenced off from everything, just the two of you. And he was saying something quietly to you, but you still didn't raise your eyes—so he talked *at you* . . . I, Marina, truly didn't want to

---

27 "*Je n'ai jamais vu de perle rose, mais je soutiens que son visage était plus perle et plus rose.*" Source unknown.

love you! But now—I don't care, because he doesn't exist for me now, but *you*, Marina, do. And now I can see it myself that he *couldn't* love you because—if he could—he wouldn't endlessly rehearse *Saint Anthony*[28]—he would be that Saint Anthony himself, or not necessarily Anthony, but in a word, a Saint...

—Yury.[29]

—Yes, yes. Generally, he'd never eat dinner or breakfast. And he'd join the Army.

—And be a Saint George.

—Yes. Oh, Marina! Yes, he'd be precisely Saint George with a spear, like on the Moscow Gates![30] He'd simply *die* of love.

And in the way she said *die* of love, it was evident that she herself—from her love of him—and of me—and of *everything*, was dying; revolution—or no revolution, rations—or no rations, Bolsheviks—or no Bolsheviks. In any case, she'd die of love, because it's her vocation—and purpose.

—Marina, will you always love me? Marina, you'll *always* love me, because I'll die *soon*. I absolutely don't know of what. I love life so, but I *know* that I'll die soon, and that's why, that's why I love everything so *madly, hopelessly*... When I say: it's Yura don't believe me. Because I know that in other cities...— Only *you*, Marina, aren't in the other cities, and—they!... Marina, have you ever thought that now, right this minute, this very little minute, somewhere in a port city or maybe on some sort of island he—the one you could love, comes up to the ship? Or maybe—he's getting off that ship. In my imagination he's always some sort of sailor, a seaman generally, an officer, or a sailor—it makes no difference... He leaves his ship and walks around the city, looking for you, who is now here, in Borisoglebsky Lane. And maybe he's now passing Third Meschansky Street. (There are awfully many seamen now in Moscow, have you noticed? In five minutes—you see so many it tires out your eyes!) But Third Meschansky Street is just as far from Borisoglebsky Lane as Singapore... (*Pause*) At school, I liked only geography—of course not all of those latitudes, longitudes, and degrees (meridians, I liked), but for the names and proper names... And the most frightening thing, Marina, is that the globe is

---

28 *The Miracle of Saint Anthony*, a play by Maurice Maeterlinck (1862–1949), a Belgian playwright, poet and essayist, who wrote in French. The play was staged by Vakhtangov Studio twice (1916, 1921), with Zavadsky in the role of Saint Anthony.

29 St. Yury is St. George.

30 St. George killing the dragon. The coat of arms of Moscow since 1781.

full of these cities and islands!—And that at every point on this globe... Do you have a globe? I'll show you if you do! I'll show you that—at every point on this globe—because the globe only looks small, and the point like a point—there are thousands and thousands of those whom I could love... (And I always say to Yura, in the same minute when I tell him I love nobody but him, I tell him, Marina... how could I say it with that same mouth, that same full mouth, that same mouth full of *him*? Because, and *this* is also true, because *both* are—true, because they're the same thing. I know it, but when I want to prove it—it's as if there's something missing in me, well—like one can't reach to the high branch, because one doesn't have that extra inch. And then it feels like I'm going crazy...)

Marina, who invented the globe? You don't know? I also don't know anything—who invented the globe or the map or the clock?—What did they teach us at school??!—Blessings on the person who invented the globe (perhaps it's some old man with a long white beard)—because of him I can immediately with my own two hands hug the whole world—with all my loved ones on it!

———

"... Or the clock..."
Once at my desk, she played with my sand clock, the children's five-minute one: inside a little wooden cage, there was a small shot glass with a constricted "waist"—and through this "waist," in the thinnest trickle—sand flowed—for five minutes.

—There's another five minutes gone... (*Then silence reigns, as if there's no Sonechka in the room, and quite unexpectedly, suddenly:*) And now there will be the last, the very last little grain! That's it!

She played with it—for a long time, frowning her little eyebrows and disappearing as a whole into this little trickle. (As I—into her.) And suddenly—a desperate cry:

—Oh, Marina! I've missed it! I suddenly—deeply—fell to thinking, and didn't turn it on time and now I'll never know what time it is. Because—imagine that we are on an island, *who* will tell us, *how* are we to know?!

—And what about a ship, Sonechka, that comes to us for the corals? For the scraps of coral?—A pirate ship, where each sailor has three watches and six watch chains! Or—even simpler: after the shipwreck the cat survived—with us. And I, even from my childhood or adolescence, know that "the Chinese see the time in the eye of cats."[31] One missionary's watch stopped working and he asked a Chinese boy on the street what time it was. The boy ran some place quickly and came back with a huge cat in his arms, looked the cat in the eye and said:—Midday.

—Yes, but what about this little trickle, the one that knew the time and was waiting for me—to turn it. Oh, Marina, I have a feeling that I've killed someone!

—You've killed the *time*, Sonechka:
What time is it? he was asked *here*,
And he replied to the curious ones—Eternity.[32]

—Oh, that's marvelous! What is it? Who is *he* and is it *true*—did it happen?

—He's a poet who went out of his mind, Batyushkov, and yes it really happened.

—It's silly to ask poets the time. It's unintelligent. That's why he lost his mind—from such stupid questions. What kind of clock is a poet? Someone needs to tell *him* what time it is and not—ask him.

—That's not it: he was already suspected of losing his mind and they wanted to check.

—And brought shame on themselves, because his response—was that of a genius, of a pure spirit. But the question—was that of a medical student. Of an idiot. So, Marina (*stroking with her pointy little finger the round sides of the small shot glass*), imagine if I were—God ... No, not that way, but the other way around, that instead of me God was holding this clock and forgot to turn it over. Well, he fell into deep pondering for a second—and ... it was *the end* of time. What a scary, what a wondrous toy, Marina. I'd want to sleep with it ...

———

A little trickle ... a little second ... Everything she said was little (*miniaturizing, imploring, touching*...), her whole way of speaking. As if her small size was passed on to it. There were words, little words, in her vocabulary, maybe an actor's and actress's, but God how different they sounded from her lips!

---

31 "*Les Chinois voient l'heure dans l'oeil des chats.*"
32 Osip Mandelstam (1891–1938), a Polish-Jewish poet and essayist, quoting Konstantin Batyushkov (1787–1855), a Russian poet, essayist, and translator.

For example, "little mannerisms": "How much I love your Alya; she's got such special little mannerisms..."

Little mannerisms (only a step, a *sign*, away from "masherochka!"[33]). No, it wasn't actress-like, but schoolgirl-like, and no wonder my ears always seemed to hear: "When I was at the Institute...."[34] The gymnasium could neither give nor take away from her this ancientness, old-fashionedness, her ancient, century-old, sense of eighteenth-century maidenhood, an urgency for adoration and genuflection, a passion for unhappy love.

A schoolgirl, then—an actress. (Or maybe, a schoolgirl, a governess, and then—an actress. I vaguely remember someone else's children...)

—When Alya asked to stay up a bit longer last night, and not to go to bed yet, she had such a moving little grimace...

Little mannerism... little grimace... little second... little trickle... and she herself was... a girl-let, which is also a diminutive...

—My father, Marina, was a violinist.[35] A *poor* violinist. He died in the hospital. I went there daily, not departing from him for a little minute. He was glad to see only me. I, in general, was his favorite.

(I'm not sure if my—memory is failing me or not when I hear: a court violinist? But a violinist of which—court? An English one? A Russian one? Because, I forgot to tell you, "Holliday" comes from the English—word "holiday"—Sunday, celebration. Sonechka *Holliday*. The name was attached to her like a bell!)

—My sisters, Marina, are beauties. I have two sisters and both are beauties. Tall, blond-haired, blue-eyed, real ladies. Only I am so plain and dark.

Why didn't they live together? I don't know. I know only that she was constantly troubled about their fate—and that this is what she paid attention to:

---

33 From French *ma chérie*, an expression used among aristocratic school girls, for whom French was often the first language, sometimes with an additional Russian endearment indicated by the suffix *-chka*.

34 The *Smolny Institute* in St. Petersburg, the first and best-known royal educational institution for young ladies of noble birth.

35 Tsvetaeva's memory is not correct in this case. Sonechka's father was a fairly famous pianist, not a violinist, and a student of A. Rubenstein. See Nic. Bernstein, "Eugène Holliday," *Musik und Theaterwelt* 41 (Berlin, 1899).

—It's necessary to have lots of money, Marina, in order for them to have *good* dresses and shoes, because they (*with a deep sign of rapture*) are beauties. They're tall, Marina, well built, only I am such a little thing.

—And you, the little one and younger,[36] must...

—Precisely because I am a little one. I, as a non-beauty, don't need a lot, but the beauties in all fairytales always need to have many things. They can't dress like me!

(A white blouse, black skirt, or white dress, I don't remember her in anything else.)

Once in some canteen or other (roach fish soup with pearl barley, second dish roach itself, no bread, Sonechka gave hers to Alya), she showed her sisters to me. They sat at a table and nodded to her from the heights of their tall English necks—blue-eyed, porcelain skin, golden-haired, in white, with a curve of grand-countess hats. She ran to them later.

—Look Alechka, you see the two ladies? They are my sisters. They're beautiful, aren't they?

—You're better.

—Ah my dear child! It's to *you* I'm better, because you love me.

—But I love you because you're the best.

Each child, disarmed by the other, became quiet.

Obviously, I was following the law of fairytales—otherwise it's hard to explain why I, with my passion for names—didn't ask their names. And so, they stayed for me, the sisters. The sisters—of Cinderella.

I remember that the *mother* was Sonechka's *responsibility*. To write to Mama.[37] To send to Mama. She must have stayed in St. Petersburg, where Sonechka herself was from. It's not for nothing *White Nights* was hers.

—You see, Marina, I know I myself walked that way, I myself loved that way. When I read it for the first time... I've *never* read it for the first time! But in *White Nights* I'm not just *she*, but also *he*, that dreamer who never got out

---

36 Sonechka was the oldest of the three sisters not the youngest, as Tsvetaeva thought.

37 Sonechka's mother, Vera Pavlovna Holliday–Rizzoni, was a daughter of the painter Pavel Rizzoni (1822–1913).

of the white night . . . You see, Marina, I'm always doubled. I'm not—doubled, but there are—two, two of me: even in my love for Yura I'm—I, and also I'm—he, Yura. I think all his thoughts before he says them. I know (that's why I'm not expecting anything!) it's funny to say: but when I'm—him—I'm too lazy to love me . . . And only with you, Marina, I'm—I, and—more I. Rather, Marina—I'm everyone who loves, walks and roams around on white nights . . . I am—a white night.

I discovered her St. Petersburg-hood immediately by the way she said "sore" instead of our Moscow "bad."

—Is it really sore?
—What?
—To say "sore." (*And she laughs.*)
—For your "sore," Sonechka, there is only one rhyme, "adore."

> Who and wherefore
> The sweet one I adore?[38]

That's how Rosanetta from my *Fortuna* (Lauzina)[39] sprang up, and that's how the whole final scene of *Fortuna* did, because in it:—"who and wherefore" is already a command to Rosanetta (Sonechka), the daughter of the porter, to be in the play:

> . . . I'm sent for your final wish.
> Maybe a letter for a loved one,
> Maybe a lock for a keepsake.
> Anything! Such a day today:
> You're allowed *anything*!

Oh, how alive Sonechka was in this—*anything*, which was uttered an hour before the execution, in this hour, which was granted, meted out, in this last love-hour and last life-hour, this before-death-hour, which held *all* the love.

All this was contained in the name—"Rosanetta."

---

38 *Fortuna* (1919) was based on Armand Louis de Gontaut, Duc de Biron (1747–1783), *Memoirs of the Duc de Lauzun*.

39 Tsvetaeva's notebook-journal # 5 (1918–1919) shows the huge impression made on her by the *Memoirs*. "Lauzuna" is the Russian feminine form of "Lauzun," a part conceived for Sonechka.

(Sonechka! I'd like, after this story of mine, for all men—to fall in love with you, all wives—to be overcome with jealousy of you, and all poets—to suffer wretchedly for you...)

In my notebooks, Sonechka began her first visit with a pitiful cry:

—Oh, Marina! (*This clever girl never added 'Ivanovna,' and just as in* White Nights, *it was the second—thousandth—time right away.*) How well I could play your Lady—in *Snowstorm*! How well I know every movement, every intonation, every break in the voice, every pause, *every* breath... And *nobody*, Marina, could play her—the way I could. But *I* can't—I'm so small.

Not in her height—not just in her height (there are enough little people!)—and her smallness was a pretty common one—like a fourteen-year-old girl. Her misfortune and her charm was that she—*was* that fourteen-year-old girl... And the year was 1919... Many times—I'm not ashamed to say it—during our short century I felt sorry that she didn't have an old, loving, and educated protector who'd hold her in his old arms as if in a silver frame... And at the same time, like a skillful navigator, would steer her... to my little boat—and a big voyage. But there was no one like that in Moscow in 1919.

(I know, I do know, that with my own love I, so to speak, "weaken" the "effect": the reader wants to do the loving himself. But I, too, as a reader, want to do the loving, just like Sonechka wants "to do the loving." I want to do the loving—like a dog. Don't you understand yet that my master is—dead and that I'm at the other end of the world and twenty-nine years away—simply howling?!)

... There was not even a trace of female coquettishness. The fervor—of a boy (along with an extremely feminine, maidenly, girlish appearance), slyness, *lutin*,[40] playfulness. Everything the Germans call *Einfall*, caprice, whimsy, fancy. (Sonechka, for you I'm robbing three dictionaries! It's a pity I don't know English—I'm sure I would find a lot of you there. And—in Spanish!...)

A few images: Natasha Rostova on the top of the flower pot, "Kiss my doll!"... Natasha Rostova[41] hugging her knees like a Hindu, and singing at the moon like a dog, was carried away from the windowsill by her singing...

---

40 A tiny mischievous fairy.
41 One of the heroines of Tolstoy's *War and Peace*.

Ogarev's Consuela saying goodbye to Herzen's Natasha near the stagecoach[42] ... Cossette with her doll, and Fantine with Cossette ... [43] All Dickens' images of maidens. And Juliet[44] ... Miry[45] ... and finally Mignona—no not Mignona but Mignon, the boy-harpist, who later become the girl Mignona, whom the youth brought home to his mother from one of his *Wanderings*, who then became Goethe himself.[46]

(I know, I'm still not giving anything and taking—a lot). Once I crossed out this part of my manuscript, but the images are crowding in, pressing me, they want—to exist once again through Sonechka...)

But the principal name—I'm concealing. It will sound only in poems—or nowhere.[47]

And that is why she—being "so small"—couldn't play any of my grown-up heroines—I had to—paint little ones. Little girls. Rosanetta in *Fortuna*, the girl in *Adventure*, Francesca in *The End of Casanova*[48]—it's all Sonechka. Sonechka alive—not whole, of course, simpler, of course, because according to Heine, a poet isn't good for the theater or the theater for a poet.[49] But she is always alive—maybe not as a whole, but it's always—she, and never: not she.

Nevertheless, one poem I've—stolen from her, who never wrote anything, never in her life wrote a line. From her, I—with my unmeasured, unparalleled honesty—yes, stole. And it's the only plagiarism of my life.

Once, telling me about some offence, she said:

—Oh, Marina! I had such big tears, they were—larger than my eyes!

---

42 Nikolay Ogarev (1813–1877), a Russian poet, historian, and political activist. His wife Natalia was Alexander Herzen's first wife, whom he called "my Consuelo" ("my consolation").

43 Cossette and Fantine, mother and daughter, are heroines of Hugo's *Les Misérables*.

44 Of Shakespeare's *Romeo and Juliet*.

45 Maybe Tsvetaeva is referring to Mirèio, a long poem by the French writer Frédéric Mistral (1830–1914), who received the 1904 Nobel Prize in Literature. The poem tells of the thwarted love of Vincent and Mireille, two young Provençal people of different social backgrounds. In her letter to her friend Solomea Andronikova (August 1930), Tsvetaeva writes that she has just finished reading the poem.

46 Mignona-Mignon, a character in Goethe's *Wilhelm Meister's Apprenticeship*.

47 Tsvetaeva's reference is unclear.

48 *Fortuna*, *Adventure*, and *The End of Casanova*; plays by Tsvetaeva.

49 Henrich Heine (1797–1856), a German poet, journalist, essayist, and literary critic. From his "Two Words about Theater" (1921).

—You know Sonechka, one day I will steal this from you and put it in my poems, because it's absolutely wonderful—it its exactness and...

—Oh, take it Marina! Everything you want—take! Take everything of mine and put it in poems, the whole of me! Because in *your* hands *everything* will be alive—forever! And what would remain of me otherwise? Just a few kisses...

And then, three years later (maybe, who knows, on the same day) a poem:

> When my dear brother
> Passed the last elm
> (mental sighs—return, come back!)
> *There were tears—bigger than eyes.*
>
> When my dear friend
> Rounded the last cape
> (mental sighs—return, come back!)
> *There were waves—bigger than arms.*
>
> Arms like to stray—from shoulders!
> Lips to follow—to enchant!
> Speech lost its sound,
> Hand its fingers.
>
> When my dear guest...
> —Dear God, please, look at us!—
> *There were tears bigger than eyes*
> *Human eyes—Atlantic stars...*[50]

(And the Atlantic stars shine above the little town Lacanau-Océan, where I—painting my Sonechka while looking at them yesterday, in the first hour of the night, remembered these lines—in reverse: at the ocean, *stars* are bigger than eyes! Here the circle closes.)

These lines were written and sent to Boris Pasternak, but their author and the addressee is—Sonechka.

And the last reflection or resonance of Sonechka in my writing—long, long after our separation, is in the refrain of my *Molodetz*[51]:—And Marusya is better than the rest! (prettier than the rest, hotter than the rest...)—Marusya

---

50 "Brothers" (1918).
51 A long fairytale in verse (1922) in which Marusya is one of female characters.

herself, who rose like a flower, surviving death itself, would give up even immortality in order to vanish together—with her beloved.

—Marina, do you think God will forgive me for kissing so many?
—You think God was counting?
—I too wasn't counting.

—And most important, I always kiss—first, just as simply as I shake hands first, only—more irresistibly. I simply can't wait! And then, every time, I tell myself:—Well, who was pushing you? It's your own fault! You see, I know very well that nobody likes it, that all of them like to bow, to beg, to look for occasions, to try to get, to hunt . . . But most importantly, I can't stand when the other kisses me—first. This way I at least know that it's what I want.

—Marina, I could never understand (and don't understand it in myself) how it's possible—just after kissing—to say a prayer. With the same lips . . . No, not the same ones! I, when I pray—never kiss and when I kiss—never pray.
Sonechka! Sonechka! From your heart's abundance *your* lips kiss!

We never kissed, except when saying hello or goodbye. But I often put my arm around her shoulders, with a gesture of defense, protection, seniority. (I was three years older. In my essence, in my whole self, older. I've never had anything little in me.)
I hugged her like a brother.
No, it was a dry fire, pure inspiration, without an attempt to discharge, squander, realize. A calamity without an attempt to relieve it. My French story addressed to one of my French male friends of fifteen years later is about that.[52] The friend is gone, but the story stays. Let *it* speak.
"I don't remember embracing her, outside the usual kisses, almost automatic, of hello and farewell. And it wasn't because of this stupid—or maybe good—*pudeur*; it was—the same as with *tu*.

---

52   The identity of this story, like that of the French friend, is unknown.

I loved her too much, all the rest was less important. Because a kiss, when one doesn't love—says a lot; when one does love—a kiss says less, and in itself is not enough. Drinking to re-drink again. A kiss when in love is seawater to a thirst. (Seawater or blood—for the shipwrecked!) If that was said before—I repeat it. The important thing isn't to say something novel, it's to find and say only what's true.

I preferred not to satisfy my thirst at all.

And one more thing that—despite its very obviousness—has certainly never been written before: a kiss when in love is a bad road, leading to the forgetting of the other. It's from the beloved, not to the beloved. It starts with kissing a soul, continues with kissing a mouth, and ends with kissing—a kiss. Annihilation.

But I often put my arms around her in a brotherly way, protectively, so as to hide her a little from life, from cold and the night. This was the Revolution for a woman—life, cold, night.

... My little one, whom I would never let go home on her own. And I simply never thought about it—because it existed—this possibility between people like us. (This impasse.) It is only now, fifteen years later, that I think, full of gratitude, for what I did not give a thought to then."[53]

Sonechka lived in a chair. In a deep dense green chair. This huge green chair surrounded, enveloped, embraced her like a forest. Sonechka lived in this green bush of a chair. The chair stood by a window, in a house on the Moscow River, surrounded by spacious vacant lots.

---

53   *Je ne me souviens pas de l'avoir embrassée hors le baiser usuel, presque machinal du bonjour et de l'adieu. Ce n'était pas de la mauvaise—ou bonne—honte, c'etait—mais la même chose qu'avec le tu: je l'aimais trop, tout était moins.*

Car un baiser, quand on n'aime pas—dit tellement plus, et quand on aime—dit tellement moins, est tellement moins. Boire pour reboire encore. Le baiser en amour c'est l'eau de mer dans la soif. (Eau de mer ou sang—bon pour les naufragés!) Si cela a déja été dit—je le redis. L'important, ce n'est pas de dire du neuf, c'est de trouver seul et de dire vrai.

J'aimais mieux garder ma soif entière.

Et—une chose qui n'a sûrement, par sa simplicité même, jamais été écrite: le baiser en amour c'est le mauvais chemin menant à l'oubli de l'autre. De l'aimé, non à l'aimé. Commençant par baiser une âme, on continue par baiser une bouche et on finit par baiser—le baiser. Anéantissement.

Mais je l'embrassais souvent de mes bras, fraternellement, protectionnellement, pour la cacher un peu à la vie, au froid, à la nuit. C'était la Révolution, donc pour la femme: vie, froid, nuit.

... Ma petite enfant que je n'ai jamais laissée rentrer seule.

Et simplement je n'y avais jamais pensé—qu'il y avait—ça, cette possibilité entre gens comme nous. (Cette impasse.) Ce n'est que maintenant, quinze ans après que j'y pense, pleine de gratitude de n'y avoir alors pas même pensé.

In this chair, she consoled herself about Yura; in it, she read my little notes; in it, she wrote me hers; in it, she learned her monologues; in it, she thoughtfully nibbled on a crust of bread; in it, after all her tears and notes, she suddenly fell asleep, sleeping through all her Yuras, Vakhtangs, and Vakhtangovs...

"It was her bed, her nest, her niche..."[54]

The walk to Sonechka's house was slightly downhill, accompanied by the noise of the dam, past the crooked fence with a sign more crooked than the posts saying, I can help correct your handwriting! (This in 1919! As if there weren't any other problems! And in addition—in such crooked letters!)

There stands the house. In the house—a chair. In the chair, Sonechka. Her legs are folded under her as if from a rising tide. (A little more and—it'll be flooded.) Her little legs jump off, her little arms stretch out to greet me:

—Marina! What happiness!

She solicitously takes my handbag and shoulder bag. Sonechka doesn't need to be convinced not to seat me in the chair: she knows the firmness of my character and habits. I sit in the window. The windowsill is wide and low. Behind it, there is—freedom. Behind my back—freedom, and in front of my eyes—love.

—Marina, I went to early mass today and cried a lot again (*counting on her little fingers in a businesslike manner*):—Yura doesn't love me, Vakhtang Levanovich doesn't love me, Evgeny Bagartionovich doesn't love me... And he could love me, at least like a daughter, because I'm—Evgenevna. Nobody in the Studio loves me.

—And—I?!

—Oh—*you* Marina, you'll *always* love me, not because I'm so good, but because you won't have time to fall out of love with me... But Yura—already has, because I myself didn't yet have time... to die.

(Love, love... What was she thinking when she repeatedly said love, love?

This reminds me of one of my own questions to an ex-soldier from the Successor's Regiment,[55] who was describing how he saved the flag:

—What did you feel while saving the flag?

---

54 "*C'était son lit, son nid, sa niche....*" Source unknown.
55 This is part of an entry from Tsvetaeva's September 1918 notebook. Some of the entries of this time became "Free Passage" and "October on the Train," which are included in Gambrell, *Earthly Signs*.

—Ah, I felt nothing: if there's a flag, there's a regiment; if there isn't, no regiment.

If there's love—there's life; if there isn't love...

Sonechka's loving was—being; not *being for the other person*, but coming true for him.)

She, the little one, squeezed herself into a ball, so her face couldn't be seen because of her hair, arms, tears. She was hiding in her own self—from everything (as our Vladimir nannie used to say about my daughter Irina:)—nestling... And around, above and below—forest, firmament, and the high tide of the chair.

From the way she pressed and squeezed herself into it, one could see how much she needed to be held in someone's big, strong, loving, older arms. (You see, a chair is—always an old man.)

The way Sonechka was in the chair, the whole lovingness of her nature could be seen. ("Nature"—is a word from *her* vocabulary, which was strangely ancient, like a translation of Dickens.) Because she squeezed into it, not like a cat into velvet, but like something alive into something alive.

I understood: she simply sat on its lap!

To entertain her a little, to divert her attention from Yura, I tell her, I recount to her, that yesterday Alya and I walked to the Vorobiev Hills,[56] and that I, in the middle of the railway bridge—sat down out of fear, seeing through the metal cross-beams—the water beneath. Alya distracted my fears with a story she made up on the spot about how the bridge gave way that minute and we fell into the water, but we didn't drown, because the angels at the last moment supported us. And they did it—because at the last minute they found out that this lady with a soldier's bag across her shoulder is—a poet, and that this girl with officer's buttons is—her daughter. And the angels took us to the fair in their arms and then rode with us on the merry-go-round. "You, Marina, rode with your angel on the lion and I with mine on the ram..." And afterwards the same angels took us to Borisoglebsky Lane,[57] and stayed to live with us, stoking the boiler and stealing wood for us... "because, the angels weren't really angels, and... you, Marina, yourself know what *kind* of angels they were..."

---

56 On the right bank of the Moscow River, one of the highest points in Moscow, giving a panoramic view of the city.

57 6 Borisoglebsky Lane, now a museum, is the house where Tsvetaeva lived with her husband, S. Efron, from 1914 to 1922.

And we, with Alya's and the angels' help, actually crossed the bridge and rode the marry-go-round: I—on the lion and she—on the ram ... And right away, for this great trip across the bridge, I buy Alya a red gelatin candy strip at the hawker's stand. And she devoutly, as if it were a host, eats it. And later two men in red shirts, in one of whom she recognizes her favorite guide from *Captain's Daughter*,[58] and not the angels, take us across the bridge, and so on—and so on ... Until Sonechka's face lit up—then—laughed—then was—radiant ...

—Marina, I played in provincial theater. And there are always fairs—in the summers in the provinces. And I love any kind of merriment with a passion. A poor merriment it was. With pink roosters and wooden blacksmiths. And I myself wore a headscarf. A pink one. As soon as I put it on—well, I had the feeling that I was simply born in it. But I have this feeling about everything, about a headscarf, about the huge white hat of my sisters... I sometimes think it could be a crown! But no, it would fall down: I have a little head: a laughably little one.—No, no, don't tell me! It's *hair*! Just try shaving it! I'm telling you there would be *nothing* left!... Marina, would you love me with my hair shaved off? But you already love me—with my hair shaved off, because in front of you everyone—has their hair shaved off, even Yurochka—has his hair shaved off, no, half-shaved: like a convict!

Marina, do I talk awfully much? Improperly much, and about everything at once, and at once—about everything? You know there's not a minute when I *don't* feel like talking, even if I'm crying: crying—sobbing hard, I still talk. I talk even while I'm asleep: I argue, tell something, prove something, and in general—like a babbling stream—I talk nonsense, Marina! After all, *nobody* listens to me. Only you!

Ah, Marina! The first person I fell in love with—was a lot older than me, more than twice my age, and his children were already grown up—I loved him for that. He was *very* lenient and never angry, but even he often reproachfully said to me jokingly:—Ah, Sonya! Don't you understand that there are minutes when talking is not necessary?

But I—continued—never stopped—never stopped talking—because everything all the time comes into my head, everything at the same time—and such different things. I'm sometimes sorry that I've only one voice to use at a time... Oh, Marina, here I talked myself into being a ventriloquist!

---

58 Pushkin's novel about Pugachev's Rebellion (1773–1775). The guide is Pugachev himself.

(Yes, she talked awfully much. My favorite words of the Tsarina in my *Tobolsk Letters*[59] are about her: The children chatter like waterfalls...)

—Now—about that fair. I walked there in my little headscarf and, looking from under it—saw: a big woman, a peasant woman, a big-as-a-tub peasant woman, in a short red skirt with sparkles—dancing to an organ-grinder. And the handle was being turned by—an ex-government clerk. He was already not so young, greenish colored, with a red nose and a cockade. (His nose was like this cockade.) I pitied him awfully: poor man, he must have been kicked out of his position for drinking, so he was doing this from—hunger! But it turned out, Marina, to be from love. Ten years before, somewhere in his town, he saw her at the fair, and she was young and slim and must have looked awfully touching. And he immediately fell in love with her (but she—didn't, because she was already married to—a ventriloquist), and from that morning he started spending all his time at the fair and when the fair left, he did too, following her everywhere. And he was kicked out of his position, and he started turning the wheel of an organ, and for ten years had been turning it, without even noticing that she had become fat—and wasn't pretty anymore, but ugly... I think if he'd stopped turning the handle, he'd have understood it all right away—and died.

Marina, I did an awful thing. You see, that woman had never kissed him—because once she had, he'd have stopped turning the organ. He was twisting and turning the kiss!—Marina!—in front of everyone, I... came to him with my heart beating:—"Don't be angry, please, but I know your story, how you gave up everything because of love, and since I myself am just like you..."—and I kissed him in front of everyone. On the lips.

Don't think, Marina, that I didn't—make myself do it. I didn't really want to. It was awkward and scary: I was afraid of him and of her, and... I simply didn't want to do it at all! But I immediately told myself:—First, tomorrow the fair is leaving town; second, today is the last chance; third, nobody has ever kissed him; fourth, nobody will ever kiss him; fifth, you always say that for you above all there's nothing superior to love; so, sixth, prove it. And—*yes*, Marina, I kissed him! This was the only difficult kiss of my whole life. But if I hadn't kissed him, I'd never have dared to play Juliet.

—And what about him? I ask.

---

[59] Part of Tsvetaeva's long poem (now lost) about Tsar Nicholas II and his family, who were executed by the Bolsheviks.

—Him (with a happy laugh)?

> Eugene stood stock still—
> As if by lightning struck...[60]

But I didn't even look. I left without turning back. Maybe—he's still standing... Ten years, ten years of dusty city squares and drunken men. Then, a kiss—but not from her!

And one more story, Marina, about Pasha-the-sailor...

Where is this story about Pasha-the-sailor? There's only a headline about him in my Spring 1919 notebook, "Sonechka Holliday's Story About Pasha-the-Sailor"—and next to it there's a blank page for writing on, but with nothing on it. Pasha-the sailor had disappeared! Pasha-the-sailor swam too far away.

Oh, a chair of stories, confessions, admissions, torments, consolations...

A second character in Sonechka's room was—a chest in chestnut-colored leather, from the time when Sonechka's father was still a court musician:

—Sonechka, what's inside?

—My dowry! (*What dowry, we'll find out later.*) Because sometime I'll definitely get married! In the most serious manner: with an offer, refusal, acceptance, with a white dress, fleurs d'orange, bridal veil...

—I hate people getting married in mufti! Simply dropping by after a quick tooth-brushing and then announcing in a month:—"We've been married a year already!" This is un-in-tel-igent. Because—there should be embarrassments and toasts, a spilling of the champagne and an I-want-to-be-congratulated—and there should be presents and—most important—there should be tears! Oh, how I'll be crying, Marina! For my Yurochka, for Eugene Bagartionovich, for the Theater, for everything, everything *that* will then have—finished: I will love only him.

The third character in Sonechka's room was—the order, which was inconceivable, unrealizable in the Revolution, as if three chambermaids worked there, dusting and sweeping. Not a speck, not a spot, nothing misplaced. Not one of (my or Yura's) little notes. Or maybe they were all under her pillow! It was the room of a schoolgirl on vacation, a governess on contract, a room from a hundred, no two hundred years ago. Or even simpler—a sailor's cabin.

---

60   Pushkin, *Eugene Onegin*.

An order not like an absence, but like a presence. In this room order lives. Like a marine guard at attention.

But nobody worked for her. Maryushka spent the whole day standing in lines for dried roach and for vegetable oil (and for one more thing about which, later!). And when she returned she beat this dried fish against the wall. Everything was done by Sonechka herself, with her own hands.

That's why I was especially affected by her friendship for me, her frank admiration of my strange, even creepy house—where everything was moved—once and for all, that is, was constantly and unceasingly moving—further and further—till it moved outside the walls, like a present, like stolen goods: like something for sale.

But I should add that all the children, especially the ones from respectable homes, always liked my house (it's the same way now) with its immeasurable freedom and... surprisingness. It is a huge *boîte à surpises*,[61] with miracles appearing right under one's feet—a giant *boîte* with an abyss for a bottom, tirelessly giving more and more new things, often without names.

Sonechka liked my house in a *childlike* way, like the fourteen-year-old child she was.

So, to complete all I have to say about my house: my house was like—Dickens's house: from *The Old Curiosity Shop*, where people slept on pilings, and a little bit from *Oliver Twist*, on sacks. Sonechka herself was—entirely—out of Dickens. She was Little Dorit—in the debtor's prison and Copperfield's Dora, with her accounting book and the dog's pagoda, and Florence with brother Dombey in her arms, and that strange girl from *Our Mutual Friend*, who called the old Jew to come up on the roof—to *not exist*:—"Come up! Come up! Die! Die!"[62]—and the one from *A Tale of Two Cities*, who plays the clavichord in a muslin tent blown by the storm, and hears the stomping of the Revolutionary mobs in the first drops of rain...

Dickens's girls—they all—existed. Because I've met Sonechka.

Sonechka's love for my house was the voice of blood: atavism.

---

61 Box of surprises.
62 Tsvetaeva quotes from the French translation: *Montez! Montez! Soyez mort! Soyez mort!*

(Dickens as transcribed by early Dostoevsky, when Dostoevsky was also Gogol: that was my Sonechka. *White Nights* has—three authors. My Sonechka was portrayed by—three authors.

So, how could she *not be able*—to do *White Nights*?)

I always came to see her in the mornings—dropped by or ran in by myself, without the children. Therefore, I remember her room always in radiance—as if there wasn't night for this room. The gold of the sun on the green of the chair and the green of the chair on the dark-gold parquet.

Ah, Sonechka! If only I could take you like this, with this chair, and carry you into—another life. Put it down, without taking you off it, in the middle of the eighteenth century—your century, when women were not required to have men's principles and were satisfied with—women's virtues, weren't required to have ideas but instead were happy with feelings, and in any case were happy—with kisses that now, in 1919, you only scare people off with.

And so from your chair those two square metal necessities would not hang, but instead—little shoes, which wouldn't step on the Moscow stones—wouldn't step at all, so that their soles would be like those of infants not yet walking.

Because you are—(I was looking for a fitting word for you, a treasure? jewel? a *joyau*? a *bijou*?)—a *Kleinod*![63] And nobody in the Moscow of 1919 sees it, except me, who can't do anything for you.

—Ah, Marina! I'm so ashamed in front of him in my low, obtuse-angled, square-nosed shoes!

"Him," this time, was not Yura. Sonechka came into my life together with my other huge misfortune: the death of Aleksey Alexandrovich Stakhovich,[64] in the first days after his death. Who was Aleksey Alexandrovich Stakhovich to me? I already told you about him somewhere and here I'll give my unpublished poem to him:

---

63   Gem (German).
64   Alexey Alexandrovich Stakhovich (1856–1919), a high-ranking Imperial Russian Chevalier Guard Regiment officer, who, in the early 1900's became a popular stage actor, associated with the Moscow Art Theatre.

Even with a hundred calluses—you can't hide three centuries!
Can't change those hands—chopping with an axe!
Oh, the most sacred of treasures:
Blue blood!—I recognize you.

Even black with ashes from the black pot—
Around you—the quietness of your Versailles.
No, even in your high-collared peasant shirt,
Your neck is not shortened!

Above the snow mounds or chimney ashes—
The other one is bent, but yours is a *proud* back!
Not by command—but by self-master's whim,
The work is given you.

Go and exchange on poor Arbat Street
A nasty herring for a pack of cigarettes—
Equality will be disturbed—by your aquiline nose:
Your nose—aquiline, the other's—snub.

But if suddenly you grow tired of receiving,
A child will offer a flower—as a tribute,
And you'll kiss her hand in the same way,
As formerly—a queen's gloved hand.

(A listener asked: "What does it mean, 'tired of receiving'?"—"It's when a person, the seller, gets tired of receiving. (*Puzzled eyes.*) Tired of receiving money; well, tired of selling."—"Does it ever happen?"—(*I playfully*) "Oh, yes. It happened with Lev Tolstoy. He grew tired of receiving the dividends from Yasnaya Polyana,[65] and the royalties from the works of Count L. N. Tolstoy, and he went to work in the fields."—"But that is an exception, a genius, while you speeek (*my interlocutor is Polish*) about a child."—"My child is a woman, and to receive, you see, is a question of patience, and women are more patient than geniuses. So, my 'child' right then gave a rose to Stakhovich.")

Second poem:

---

65 Tolstoy's family estate, southwest of Tula, and now a museum. Tolstoy was born in the house, where he wrote both *War and Peace* and *Anna Karenina*. He is buried nearby.

> Not from locked-with-seven-locks bakeries,
> And not from frozen stoves—
> You went to your grave, a Russian master,
> With a master's stride, your shoulders straight.
>
> The old world was on fire—fated.
> —Nobleman, give way—to woodcutter!
> The mob was blooming, but around you
> The air of the eighteenth century breathed.
>
> And the mob de-roofed castles,
> Straining for the desired loot—
> "*Bon ton, maintien, tenue*," you taught the boys—
> To the accompaniment—of a crashing Universe.
>
> You didn't meet them with a bread-salt welcome,
> Your ravishing hands—from noble boredom!—
> With the black kingdom of working calluses—
> Were intercrossed.

(I'm not one to despise calluses—I'd have to despise myself first—but back *then* calluses were thrust upon us and imposed on us as a duty of love. So that's where the hate comes from.)

I'll add one more thing: Sonechka and Stakhovich were in the same Theater Studio—Number Two—where Sonechka's *White Nights* was staged with only one character—Sonechka, and *The Green Ring*,[66] with only one character—Stakhovich (the ring is the youth).

Now Sonechka told me about those lessons, "*bon ton, maintien, tenue*,"[67] mentioning her obtuse-nosed boots:

—It was such shame, Marina! I burnt with it every time! For example, Stakhovich explains how one is supposed to bow to a woman, to give your hand to her, or how to see someone off, or the opposite, how to receive a person: "Do you understand? Well, let's have someone show it. Nobody can? Perhaps you, Holliday, Sonya." And I walk on, Marina, burning with shame for my

---

66 A four-act play by Zinaida Gippius (1869–1945), a Russian poet, playwright, and novelist.
67 Good manners or style, good bearing, good grooming or comportment.

crude, low, awful boots with ox-like muzzles. To walk in such boots through the whole dance hall—in front of him, who danced in all the court ballrooms, who's used to such elegant shoes ... and little feet ...

These little feet! Alas! On what far strand
Do you of spring the blossoms crush?[68]

But I come out, Marina, because otherwise—nobody else would, because the others are—worse. Not in the way they're dressed, but ... well, in their way of knowing how ... to give a hand, let the guest go. Oh, how well I could have done it all, Marina—if not for my shoes! How from birth I deeply, deeply know it all and can do it! How I recognize—everything—immediately!

And he was always pleased with me, maybe because he wanted to console me for those horrible boots?: "Yes, yes, exactly—this way." And he never looked at them, as if he didn't see how they *burned* me. And I didn't look at them either, because I was only afraid *before*, before he said: "Well, maybe you—Holliday, Sonya!" And when he said it—that was the end. I walked freely and didn't think of them—Oh, Marina, I didn't condescend to think of them.

But he saw them—very well, because when one of our female students complained that she couldn't do something because "her boots were too heavy," he replied, "Whatever shoes one's wearing, there's still the stride. Look at Sophia Evgenevna. Who could tell that on each of her little feet is a ton[69] of iron, like on the prisoner Bonivard?"[70]

—Sonechka, do you know the fairytale about the Little Mermaid?

—The one who danced on the knives? But it's a thousand times easier than on the irons! Because they are heavy irons ... Percherons.[71] It's my most favorite fairytale, Marina! Every time I read it I feel that I'm—her. How much she wanted to rise up to the surface—and how she did rise up, and saw the upper world, and this marble boy who turned out to be dead, and ... a prince, and how she made him come alive. But she became mute—and, though mute, she afterwards danced in front of him on the knives ... Oh, Marina, it's—the

---

68 Pushkin, *Eugene Onegin*.
69 Literally, a *pood*, an old Russian measure weighing approximately 16.38 kg.
70 The *Prisoner of Chillon* (1816), a narrative poem by Byron, chronicling the imprisonment of a Genoese monk, François Bonivard.
71 Literally, a *bityug*—A Russian breed of carthorse.

highest bliss—to love that way, to love that way... I'd give my soul, to be able to give my soul!

Ah, Marina! How much I love—to love! How madly I love—to love! From morning, no, from before morning, in that same before-morning—still asleep, but already still knowing... Do you ever forget, when you love—that you love? I—never do. It's like a toothache—only contrary—a contrary toothache. Only there it aches, but here—I'm at a loss for words... (*after thinking a bit*)—it sings. Well, it's like sugar being contrary to salt, but with the same force. Ah, Marina! Marina! Marina! What wild fools they are.

—I (*somewhat, surprised:*) Who?

—Well, those who *don't* love, don't themselves love, as if the point is for *you* to be loved. I'm not saying, of course... one gets tired when one hits a wall. But you know, Marina (*mysteriously*), there's no such wall that I *couldn't* get through. Even Yurochka... at some moments... has almost loving eyes! But he—I have a feeling—has no strength to say it. It's easier for him to pick up a mountain than to say the word. Because he has nothing to support it with. But for me, behind that mountain—there's another and another and another...—a whole Himalayas of love, Marina! Do you notice, Marina, how all of them, even the most kissing ones, even those who seem so loving, are afraid to say the word and how they *never* say it?! One explained to me that it's... crude (*chuckles*)... old-fashioned, and: why speak words when there are—actions? (That is, kisses and so on.) But I said to him—"Hey! No! The actions don't prove anything, while the word proves—everything." You see, this is all I need from a person: "I lo-ove you," and nothing else. Let them do whatever they like afterward, and in whatever way not love me, I won't believe in their actions, because the word—existed. And I was fed only on this word, Marina, that's why I became so thin.

Oh, how miserly, thrifty, and cautious they are, Marina! I always want to tell them: "Just say it. I *won't*—check." But they don't say it, because they think it means—marriage, tying themselves down and not untying. If I'd said the word first, I'd never leave first. (But they don't even say it second, Marina, or any other time.) As if it's possible with me—*not* to be the first to leave!

Marina! I—never in my life—left first. And in my entire life—as much as God gives me—I won't leave first. I simply *can't*. I always wait for the other to leave. I do everything to help him leave first, because for *me* to leave first is—like stepping over my own corpse. (What a horrid word. Absolutely dead. Ah, I understood: this is the dead whom nobody ever loved. But for me there aren't such dead, Marina!) I, even in my inner self, never left first. I've never stopped loving first. I always stay—to the last possible moment, to the last drop—the drop one drinks in childhood, when it's already hot from the emptiness of the glass, but you still suck, and there's only your own breath!

Ah, you know, you'd laugh—it was a very short encounter—during a tour—there was a very young man, it doesn't matter who. I fell madly in love with him, because all evening he was sitting in the first row—and was *poorly* dressed, Marina! He sat not according to his means, but to his eyes. And on the third evening, he looked at me as if—either his eyes would jump out, or he himself—would jump onto the stage. (I'm talking, moving, and at the same time glancing: well, how is he doing? no, still sitting.) But this has to be understood! Because it wasn't the usual male-in-love, *eating-you-up* stare (he was almost a boy)—it was a drinking-you-up stare. Marina, he looked enchanted, as if I, with every word and movement—as if on a string—on a rope—pulled him closer, reeled him in. It was the feeling the mermaids must know and also—violinists, rather their bows—and rivers . . . and fires, Marina! . . . As if he'd jump into me any minute—like into a fire. I don't know how I was able to carry on. Because all this time, Marina, *I* had a feeling that I, sooner or later, would stumble—into him, into those eyes.

And when I was finally behind the curtains (I know, it's awfully vulgar, but *everything* is vulgar as soon as it has a *location*, and the *rocks* on which the maidens of D'Annunzio[72] sat—aren't much better!) . . . so behind those unlucky curtains, I kissed him, but I felt nothing, except one thing: I was saved!

. . . It lasted an awfully short time. We had nothing to talk about. At first, I was talking, talking, talking, and afterward—I became quiet. For it's impossible, I—can't, when in response to all my words—there are only eyes, only kisses! So, in the morning, before-the-morning, I'm still sleeping, well partly awake, I suddenly notice that I'm repeating something all the time—yes, my lips are moving, making words . . . I listened to what I was saying—and you know what it was:—Please, let me like you a *bit* more! Just a little more, a minute longer, a second longer—let me like you!

—Well, and?

—No. He *couldn't*.

—He couldn't what?

---

72 Gabriele D'Annunzio, an Italian poet, playwright, orator, journalist, and soldier (1863–1938), in his poem, "The Maidens of the Rock."

—Make me like him more. He couldn't—even if he'd heard it. Because don't think: I was asking him while he was sleeping—we lived in different places . . . and in general—I was asking the air, maybe—asking God. I simply begged, Marina, I begged myself, to draw it out a little longer.

—Well, and . . . ?

—(*With shining eyes*:) I did it! He—couldn't, but I—could! He never found out. Everything was proper. And his strict father-general in Moscow didn't even know I was an actress: and he thought I was at a girlfriend's. (But what if he had suddenly followed me and become a lighting technician?) I'll never forget it (*this* I didn't make up): when the train started moving—because I don't ever kiss in public—I kissed *his* roses in the window. Because, Marina, love is—love, but justice is—justice. It's not his fault that I stopped liking him. It's not a fault, but a misfortune. It's not *his* fault, but *my* misfortune: my unintelligence. It's like breaking a china set and then being angry that it wasn't made of metal.

And the play, during which we fell in love, was by Yury Teary.[73] Funny name? Perfect for me. Even our impresario said to me: "Little Sonechka, you're always crying, you should marry this Yury Teary." (*In a business-like manner*:) Do you know Marina, is he an old man?

(I know I'm breaking the unity of the tale, but honor is—higher than art. This "let me like you a little longer!" is—my second plagiarism.

> As that consumptive woman,
> Moaned in the night:
> Let me like you longer!

And, further:

> As that consumptive woman,
> Who begged everyone: let me like you
> A *little* longer! . . .

And, finally:

> That woman with the sailor—
> Life, I bargain with you:
> One minute *longer* let me like you! . . .[74]

---

73 Yury Lvovich Slezkin (1885–1947), a Russian writer. Sleza means "tear."
74 From Tsvetaeva's poem "The Last Sailor."

In this way gradualness is presented and preserved through the verses, having expressed Sonechka's request to *the end*. For if Sonechka had been older, she'd have ended up—this way.)

—Well, Sonechka, tell me more about Stakhovich. What else were his lessons about besides bowing?

—About everything. For example, how to do one's hair. "A woman's hairdo should give, guard, and preserve the form of her head. There shouldn't be any superstructures. The hair should only and *exactly* frame the face, so the face will remain the most important thing. The hair should be parted straight and smoothly combed back half-covering an ear: like yours—Holliday, Sonya."—"Alexey Alexandrovich! But mine isn't very smooth!"—I respond laughing. "Yes, but those are natural curls, because you have a natural wave, and the *frame* is still there, but it's just a bit rococo . . . I'm talking about the general line. You have it simple and beautiful, simply beautiful." (Oh, Marina, how proud I was in those moments! Because I felt that not only from these in front of him, but also from all those *behind* him too, he singled me out!) . . . And also, for example, about how to behave when you walk in the street and your stocking falls down or something else gets untied: "It doesn't matter whom you're walking with, you should calmly move aside and without hurry, without any rush, correct, fix the disorder . . . You shouldn't be tearing at anything or rushing anything, not even especially hiding: calm, do it calm-ly, calm-ly . . . Holliday, please show us! You and I are walking together on Arbat Street and you feel that your stocking is falling down, three more steps and it will be down all the way . . . What would you do?" I demonstrate. I move aside, a bit away from him, bend, grope for the elastic and calm-ly, calm-ly . . . "Bravo, bravo, Holliday, Sonya! If you could really do that with *any* companion and not just with me, (*here his lips fold into a marvelously pitiful and derisive smile, Marina*!) an old teacher, and preserve such composure . . ."

Once I couldn't help myself and asked: "Alexey Alexandrovich, how do you know it all, about falling stockings, ribbons, our feelings, and heads? How do you know us so well from head to toe?" And he, seriously (serious enough for everyone else to believe, but for me not to do so) replied: "The fact that I know everything isn't surprising. I'm an old person. But how is it that such questions come to a little girl like you?" But always, always *I* showed—it was shown on me—how to do it, on the others—how *not* to do it, but on me—how to. The boys called me: Stakhovich's show-case.

—Were the girls—jealous?

—(*She, triumphantly:*) Exploding with jealousy!! You see, it was such an honor! Everyone there loved him madly, and if you only knew what kind of matryoshkas[75] they were! And, in addition, obnoxious, over-dressed ones! And—with what curls! (*Chuckles.*) But *they* had real shoes, lady's ones.

—But why, Sonechka, do you make so little money?

—(*She, meekly:*) The others have husbands, Marina. Some have one husband and some two. And I have—only Yura. And Mama. And two sisters, you know, they are . . .

—Beauties. I know, I saw. And you are—Cinderella, who has to clean the ashes while the others dance. But the actress is—you.

—But they are—older. No, Marina, after Papa's death I understood it all, and—decided. And *them* (*showing me her little foot*) I nevertheless hate. How many tears they cost me at first! I couldn't get used to them.

———

—Marina! It was awful. When Stakhovich first came back to the Art Theater after having typhus—nobody recognized him. They simply—passed by without recognizing him, he was so changed, aged. And then he said to one of our students: "I'm just a superfluous old man."

. . . And how he sang, Marina! He had such a marvelous voice! (*We were sitting on the top floor in our deserted wooden kitchen, the children were asleep, there was a moon . . .*)

> Yes, there was a waltz, old-fashioned, languid,
> Yes, that was a wondrous . . .

(*she cuts it short, as if to put a full stop*)
—waltz![76]

> If I were young,
> How much I'd love you!

---

75 A set of Russian nested dolls. Here it means "crudely dressed," as these dolls were often crudely painted.

76 "I Remember the Sound of a Marvelous Waltz," a popular Russian song; music and lyrics by N. Listov.

"Alexey Alexandrovich! The last part is—yours! Those words aren't in this song!" we said to him, laughing. He replied: "They are in mine!"

Why, Alexey Alexandrovich, knowing the value of—women—and pearls—and souls, didn't you fall in love with my Sonechka, and love her more than your own soul? You saw around her "the air of the eighteenth century."[77] *What* was missing, that you could not live through that horrid March day?[78] *What* couldn't you handle—one more hour without?

And she was nearby—alive, delightful, ready to love and to die for you—and dying without love.

Maybe you thought: she had her own young admirers... Yes, I saw ones like that! And so did—you.

How could you leave her to—all, each, any of those boys you were so fruitlessly teaching "*bon ton, maintien, tenue*"?

However, there was one among them... But about him—more later.

They didn't like her in the Theater: they—passed her over. I often complained about it to my friend Vakhtang Levanovich Mchedelov[79] (Sonechka's director, the one who discovered her for Moscow).

—Marina Ivanovna, don't think it's easy: she's very difficult. Not that she's capricious, but somehow, she's discourteous. One never knows how she'll take one's comment. Sometimes, she is—inappropriately giggly (he himself was—a deep melancholic). You tell her something, but she looks into your eyes and—laughs. And she laughs in such way that it—makes you smile. And that's the end of—the lesson. And the end of—your prestige. What do you do

---

77 Tsvetaeva is quoting her own poem to Stakhovich.
78 On March 10, 1919, outraged by the atrocities committed by the Bolshevist regime and suffering from severe depression, Stakhovich committed suicide by hanging.
79 Vakhtang Levanovich Mchedelov (born Mchedlishvili) joined the Moscow Art Theater in 1904, first as an assistant to Stanislavsky. When the school closed for financial reasons in 1916, Mchedelov started collecting money for a new project, which finally materialized as the Moscow Art Theater, Second Studio.

about it? And she isn't—ambitious, oh not at all, but she is—power-loving, autocratic: *she* knows how to do it—her way or—no way.

—But maybe she really knows, and that it really has to be—that way?

—Then she needs to have her own theater. However, we have—a studio, teamwork, a few attempts . . . we try to reach things together.

—What if she reached them the day she was born?

—Hmm . . . In *White Nights*—yes. In general, she's an actress for herself, for her own height, her own voice, her own laugh, her own tears, her own braids . . . She's *exceptionally* gifted, but I still don't know whether this gift is of—an actress, a human being, or a woman . . . She's—all of her—too exceptional, too much of—an exception, unusable in an ensemble: she's the only one people look at!

—Give her main roles!

—But that's not always possible. And—for purely external reasons—she isn't good for every role—she's so little. For her, things have to be specially—staged. You have to put her in the middle of the stage—and that's it. Like in *White Nights*. She knows everything, wants everything, and can *do* everything—on her own. What is a director supposed to do? (*Me, to myself:* "Kowtow.") And besides, we're a studio and there is such thing as elementary justice. There should be a chance for others to—show themselves as well. She's an actress of the western theater, not of the Russian. For her separate plays should be written . . .

—Vakhtang Levanovich, you have in your hands—a miracle.

—And what am I supposed to do with it when it's *not*—needed?

—If you don't need it—give her into good hands!

—But where are they?

—I'll tell you using your own—indictment: The hands of the eighteenth century, the hands of a young melancholic English gentlemen and patron—the hands in which he'd carry her—in the hours when he wasn't in front of her on his knees. What is she missing? Only two past centuries, two mighty loving hands, and her own pinkish shell—the theater. Don't you see that she's—a child-actress, an actress in a gold carriage, a bird-actress? Malibran,[80] Adelina

---

80   Maria Malibran (1808–1836), a Spanish mezzo-soprano.

Patti,[81] a *oiseau-mouche*,[82] and not a student of your Second or Third Studio? She should be *adored* not *abhorred*.

—Nobody's abhorring her—though she herself is capable of it! You don't even know how sharp-toothed, porcupine-like, uncomfortable, somehow non-portable she is . . . Maybe a—beautiful soul, but a—horrible personality. Marina Ivanovna, don't be angry, but you, actually—don't know her. You know her only poetically, humanly, in your home, with you nearby. But there's a professional life, a life of comradery. I wouldn't say that she's a bad comrade, because she's simply—no comrade at all; she's on her own. Do you know Stanislavsky's "entering into the circle"?[83] Well, our Sonechka is—continuously exiting from the circle. Or, which is the same thing, is—its absolute center.

And she has a—surprisingly sharp tongue! If there's even a little joke at her expense—she cries. She cries, but right away—says something venomous. One doesn't ever know whether she is a child, a woman, or a devil. Because she can be a real devil!

(That second it dawned on me: one doesn't talk this way about unloved ones, but only about those: one loved in vain or loved previously! But nobody talked about her—any differently. For all of them she remained—an obstacle. And as an obstacle—no one loved her.)

—Marina! Today I'm awfully unfortunate.

—Is it our mutual angel again?

—No, this time it's not him, but the opposite! Our studio decided to stage *Four Devils*,[84] and gave me not one, not even the fourth, not even the tiniest one, the fifth one! (*Here she said something unforgettable:*) I had such big tears. They were bigger than my eyes!

---

81 Adelina Patti (1843–1919), an Italian-French soprano.
82 Hummingbird.
83 Konstantin Sergeievich Stanislavsky (1863–1938), inventor of the famous method of training actors.
84 Perhaps Sonechka is referring to *A Tale about Ivan-the-Stupid, His Two Brothers, Semen-the-Warrior and Taras-the-Big-Belly, and an Old Devil and Little Devils*, by Michael Chekhov (1891–1955), based on Tolstoy's fairytale, in which Sonechka at first got the role of the youngest devil (named One), but afterward had the role taken away from her (Galina Brodskaya, *Sonechka Gollidei. Zhizn' e akterskaya sud'ba*, 273).

Yes, they thought her mean. They didn't say it openly to me, because they thought me—even meaner. But in response to my being moved by her kindness—they were ruminant or—mumbled something. I've never seen more simple, obvious, and glaring kindness being someone's whole essence. She gave everything away, understood everything, took pity on everyone. And her—"meanness"? It was just like Khodasevich's[85] and mine, sometimes a question, or to be more exact—an answer, and even more exact—a *riposte* due to a linguistic gift, a kind of linguistic *exchange*—a cat's paw.

An exemplary little girl, a Good Little Devil. My little Sonechka—my immense Sonechka—entirely resembled Countess de Ségur.[86] They were not fellow countrymen for nothing!

(Comtesse de Ségur—a great writer, had the silly whim to imagine herself a grandmother, and wrote only for children. Please note her *New Fairy Tales* (Bibliotheque Rose)—the best and the least known of all the things she wrote. These fairytales are absolutely exceptional, because they are absolutely individual, without any borrowing—even from folktales. These fairytales, to which I've been devoted for four decades, I've given as presents four times here in Paris, and rescued three times, because for me to see them in a shop window is—inevitably—to buy them.)

Two last words about Vakhtang Levanovich Mchedelov—so as not to be unjust. He deeply loved poetry, was a real friend to me, and a person of true humanity. I endlessly preferred him to the splendid Vakhtangov (Sonechka's "Yevgeny Bagartionovich") from whom toward me there wafted or blew— a cold head breeze, of the sort a philistine calls "an eccentricity." It was the coldness and barrenness of the very word "eccentricity." (I may be mistaken in theatrical terms, but in human terms—no.) And if Vakhtang Levanovich couldn't do something for my Sonechka, it's because that *something* was *everything*, that is to say, an entire destruction of himself, of everything,

---

85 Vladislav Felitsianovich Khodasevich (1886–1939), an influential Russian poet and literary critic, who presided over the Berlin circle of Russian émigré litterateurs.

86 *Petite fille modèle—et Bon petit Diable. Toute ma petite Sonechka—immense—tenue dans la C-tesse de Ségur. On n'est (pas) compatriotes pour rien!* Sophie Rostopchine, Comtesse de Ségur (1799–1874), was a French writer of Russian birth, best known today for her novel *Sophie's Misfortunes*, intended for children. One of her fairytales was titled *Un Bon Petite Diable—A Good Little Devil* (1865).

nothingness, of love. That was, publicly, an appalling injustice. Vakhtang Levanovich was unarguably a better person than I, but I loved Sonechka more. Vakhtang Levanovich loved theater more; I loved Sonechka more. And why wouldn't he give her "at least the smallest, at least the fifth devil,"—maybe these devils weren't real ones, but allegorical devils and so not really devils at all? (It's very doubtful that there would be four caudate devils in a row on stage—in all four acts.) I don't know this play, but it seems to me that it's—from the circus novel of Herman Bang, *Four Devils*.[87] I was just insulted because of the word "mean." And—her tears.

No, they didn't love my Sonechka. The women—because of her beauty, the men—because of her intellect, the actors (*mâles et femelles*)—because of her gift, and all of them—because of her uniqueness: the danger of uniqueness.

> All women found her ugly,
> But all men were crazy about her.[88]

The first—yes (that is, in the poem—but she was exactly the opposite), the second—no. In the full bloom of her beauty, gift, and inner fire—nobody loved her, they spoke about her with a smirk ... and with caution.

For men she was a dangerous ... child. A creature, not a woman. They didn't know how to deal with her ... They weren't able ... (Sonechka's intellect was never asleep. "Sleep my right eye, sleep my left eye ... ," but the third one—was never asleep.[89]) They were all afraid that she (when she cried with tears!) was laughing—at them. When I recall *the ones* they preferred to my Sonechka, what falsity, what fakeness, what pseudo-femininity—from pseudo-

---

87 Herman Joachim Bang (1857–1912), a Danish author, part of the so-called Modern Breakthrough. A film based on his Four Devils appeared in 1928. Tsvetaeva is right to hesitate about which play Sonechka is referring to. There is no evidence of the Second Studio's having staged Bang's play in 1919.

88 *Toutes les femmes la trouvent laide,*
Mais tous les hommes en sont fous ...
A French proverb.

89 The reference is to a Russian fairytale, "The Tiny Little Havroshechka," in which there are three wicked sisters, a one-eyed one, a two-eyed one, and one with three eyes. Havroshechka tries to put them to sleep to save her cow, but she forgets about the third eye.

Beatrice to pseudo-Carmen. (Let's not forget that in the theater we are at the very heart of falseness).

By the way, she was more a little Spanish girl than a little English one, and if I said that there was no nationality to her, it's in order to protect her from what—in her case—was the first one thrust upon her—the Small Russian one, which is the most typical nationality. The faces of Spanish women—the least national of all nationalities—present the most latitude for the human face in its unity and individuality: from portrait to—allegory, a Spanish female face is a human female face with all its possibilities of suffering and passion, it is—Sonechka's face.

But I mean—a little geographically Spanish woman, not an operatic one. A little street Spanish woman, a worker in a cigarette factory. Set her down like a spinning top in the middle of Seville's square—and she will—belong there. It's not for nothing that I, without thinking about what I'm writing now, in the heat of the moment and right away, in my first poems to her, called her: "A Tiny Cigarrera!" And then—even better: Consuela—or Conchita, Concha! Concha, after all, is—almost Sonechka!—Oh, yes, Marina! Oh, no, Mariana! Concha—you see is something that will end, but even sooner![90]

And it was not for nothing that the first thing I heard about her was—Infanta. (From Infanta to Cigarrera—a Spanish female face is the most classless face.)

Now, when Spain is closer to us, the real Spain moved closer[91] and the pseudo-Spain moved away. When every day we see dead and alive women's and children's faces, we can find Sonechka's face among them: one only has to look among the fourteen-year-olds. With a correction—for her uniqueness.

I'll say one more thing: such little faces sometimes bloom in the lower middle class.[92] In the Russian lower middle class. They bloomed in the Russian lower middle class in—Turgenev's time. (Everything in late Turgenev is—under their influence.) Muslin curtains and behind them—huge black eyes. ("Whom does she resemble? The whole family is—blond.") Such faces were found among youngest sisters—the seventh one after the sixth, the last one: "The postman had six daughters. The seventh was a beauty..."

---

90   In Russian *konchittsya* means end, death.
91   Tsvetaeva is talking about the Spanish Civil War (1936–1939).
92   A social class that comprised various categories of townspeople, such as craftsmen, tradesmen, and small householders.

In small sloboda settlements...[93] In the backwoods... In the outskirts... There where the ends—don't meet. Earrings—go well with such faces.

And also—nuts. Sonechka passionately loved nuts, and missed them most of the now-unavailable foods. In her laughter, in her teeth, in her speech was a touch of cracked and rolling-away nuts, as if the whole of a squirrel's supply was rolling everywhere: "The green ones, if you stick your teeth in them—are sour, the sourest there are. Sourer than a lemon! Sourer than a green apple! And suddenly—there is the nut itself: creamy and slightly tan on the bottom. The kernel so round and firm—the firmest there is—jumps in half as if cut by a knife! Two halves, one for you and the other for me. But I don't just like hazelnuts (I like to gather them, Marina! When they're above you—a whole cluster, more and more, and you can't reach it, so you bend and bend the branch down, and—suddenly it gets away from you and swings up high—into the blue again—such blue that your eyes are alight, such green that your eyes hurt!—you know, they're like stars, Marina, and the pods are like sunrays!), I like city nuts too, and walnuts, and peanuts, and pine nuts, such marvelous little black babies... a whole bag! And I like to read *War and Peace*. I love—*Peace*, Marina, but *War*—I don't. And so always—by accident—I skip many pages. Because it's a male thing, Marina, not ours."

... And from nuts rolling, a brook on pebbles—the eddies on the pebbles, the pebbles under the stream—from the chatter of leaves ("The wind flips the birch tree leaves"[94]...), and pearls gently squeezed in the palm—and greenish lilies-of-the-valley, and even—from the flood of tears!—from all that is round and moving in nature, in all that laughs, all that nature laughs with, Sonechka laughed. But since it was done all together with the leaves, the water, the peas, the nuts, and—with her white teeth and her black eyes too—it turned out incomparably richer than in nature.

... In a word:

---

93   A *sloboda* was a kind of Russian settlement in Belarus and Ukraine. The name is derived from the early Slavic word for "freedom" and may be loosely translated as "tax-free settlement."

94   Tsvetaeva believes that she quotes this line from the poem of V. V. Kazin (1898–1981), but the journals of I. N. Rozanov (1872–1959), a historian of Russian poetry, indicate that it is not his, and Kazin himself didn't remember these lines.

> I'd be listening to this chatter
> I'd be kissing these little feet....[95]

Men didn't like her. Women—either. *Children* loved her. Elderly people. Servants. Animals. Very young maidens.

Everything, she was given everything, in order to be senselessly, soullessly, on someone's lap—beloved: a gift, a fire, a beauty, an intellect, an inexplicable charm, and this nameless fame—better than the named one ("the one of—*White Nights*..."), and all of that in her hands was—ashes—because she herself wanted to love. To love someone herself.

There should have been a poet for Sonechka. A major poet, that is, as major a human being as a poet. She didn't meet one. Maybe one of the first two hundred volunteers in Novocherkassk in 1918.[96] Any one of the two hundred. But in Moscow of 1919 there were none. There were none of them—anywhere anymore.

—Oh, Marina! How much I loved them! And how I cried about them! And how I prayed for them! You know, Marina, when I love—I'm scared of nothing. I don't feel the earth under my feet! Everyone said to me: "Where are you going? You'll be killed! That's where there's the—most shooting!"

But I went there every day bringing dinner in a basket, because, you see, one has to eat?

And I went through rows of Red Army soldiers to get there: "Where are you going, my beauty?"—"I'm bringing dinner to my sick mother, she was left across the Moscow River."—"We know such sick mothers! With a moustache and a beard!"—"Oh, no, I don't like the bearded-mustachioed ones: mustachioed is—a cat, bearded—a goat! I'm *truly* going to my mother!" (By now I'm crying.)—"Well, if that's the truth, to mother, then pass, pass. But look out, God forbid—you'd be killed by a bullet, either ours or the cadets, and your old mother have to go without her dinner."

---

95   From Pushkin's poem, "If not for the vague attraction...."
96   The Don Volunteer Army belonged to the short-lived Don Republic and was a part of the White Movement in the Russian Civil War.

I still walk by the Church of Christ the Savior with a special feeling, that's *where* I brought them dinner, my little pigeons.

—Marina! I lie awfully sometimes! And I believe it—myself. Like yesterday when I stood in line, I got talking to a soldier—a good one: he was waiting for the same thing we were. First, we talked about prices and then about something more important, something seeerious (*her pronunciation*).

—How smart you are, Miss, despite your young age. You know about everything, you know the *truth* about everything...

—But I'm not a Miss at all! My husband is with Kolchak![97] I tell him. I talk to him and I cry with real tears—because I love my husband so and I'm afraid for him, and because I know he won't make it to Moscow—and because I *don't* have a husband who's on the march with Kolchak...

Sonechka adored my children: six-year-old Alya and two-year-old Irina. The first thing she did when she came was—take Irina out of her gated crib.

—How are you, my little girl? Do you recognize your Hallidah? How do you sing about me? Halli-dah, Halli-dah! Yes?

Irina is on her lap and Alya is under her wing—under the right, free-from-holding Irina, arm. ("I *always* carry children on my left, don't you? So as to protect them with my right. And to hug them.") This is how I see the trinity: a group of three heads frozen in motionless bliss. Irina's high-foreheaded one (I almost said—high-horned), with high large sheep-like bright-gold curls on her forehead. Alya's pale-gold one, like the small helmet of a little knight. And between them—Sonechka's smooth-curled, chestnut one, which was sometimes frozen in the bliss of a perfect embrace and sometimes diving back and forth from one to the other. And a funny thing—Sonechka's grown-up one didn't seem much bigger than the two children's:

> The mother who spawned you
> Was an early rose:

---

97 Alexander Kolchak was the "Supreme Ruler" of the White movement (1918–1920).

> She dropped a petal—
> When she gave you birth.[98]

(Only when I remember Sonechka do I understand all comparisons of a woman to flowers, eyes to stars, lips to petals, and so on... —into the depths of time.

Not only understand, but recreate.)

... That's how they're imprinted in my memory—as a group. As if it was already—a photograph.

At times, when Irina was asleep and Sonechka was sitting with Alya already on her lap, it was a perfect vision of Florence with Dombey-brother: Dickens's heart would have stood still if he had seen these two![99]

Sonechka with my children was the most perfect vision of motherhood, a maiden's motherhood, a motherhood of maidenhood: a maiden, no—a girl God-mother:

> Above her firstborn is the God-mother:
> This, you see—doesn't compute![100]

—Well now, enough about Hallidah, otherwise I'll get conceited! Let's sing "Ay-Doo-Da" (*to Alya and, under her breath, to me*: it's almost the same thing![101]). Well, how do you sing it?

> —Ay-doo-da, ay-doo-da
> There's a clow on the oak
> He is paing tlum-pet.
> Tlum-pet, tlum-pet.

---

98   From a poem "Being in love," by Konstantin Dmitriyevich Balmont (1867–1942), a Russian symbolist poet and translator. He was one of the major figures of the Silver Age of Russian Poetry and a close friend of Tsvetaeva.
99   Florence and Dombey-brother (Paul) are characters in Dickens, *Dombey and Son*.
100 Source unknown.
101 Because *Hallidah* and *ay–doo-da* rhyme.

—Yes, that way, good girl! Only there's another part to it:—"Trumpet molded, trumpet golden..." But that's too hard for you, that's for when you're a bit older.

And so on for hours, never tired or bored, never running dry.

—Marina, I'll never have children.

—Why?

—I don't know, the doctor told me and explained it all, but it's so complicated, all our insides...

She's serious, like a grown-up, with eyelashes already glimmering, like the points of stars.

And there wasn't a bigger misfortune for her than to come to my children empty-handed.

—There's nothing, nothing today, my little girl! (*she responds to Irina's appalling-appealing eyes*). I, you understand, was waiting till the last minute, hoping that they'd issue supplies... But they didn't—because they're nasty—and killed the Tsar, and left my Irina hungry... But to make it up to you I promise, you understand, that, without fail, next time I'll bring something for you and also some sugar.

—Sugal give! (*joyfully imperious*).

—Irina, you should be ashamed of yourself! (*Alya says indignantly, ready to clasp Irina's mouth shut with her hand out of embarrassment.*)

And Sonechka's detailed explanation—in response to Irina's understanding nothing but "sugar"—that sugar is—tomorrow, and that tomorrow is—when Irina will go to bed at night, and then she'll wake up again and Mama will wash her face and her little hands, and then she'll give her some potato and...

—Potata give!

—Ah, my dear little girl, I don't have any potatoes today either, I'm talking about tomorrow (*Sonechka says, with genuine embarrassment*).

—Sonechka! (*Alya, says excitedly*) one shouldn't talk about food with Irina, because she understands it very well, it's all she understands, and from now on she'll be asking for it!

—Oh, Marina! How much I grieved that I won't have any children, and now—it seems—I'm happy about it: because it's such a horror, simply a horror. I'd go mad if my child asked and I had nothing to give... However, there are still the children of others.

There were no "of others" for her—neither children nor people.

Two entries from Alya's diary of the spring of 1919 (six years old):
"The evening came, I already started washing. Suddenly I heard knocking. With my face still wet and Marina's silk shawl thrown on, I quickly went down and asked: Who's there? (Marina knew this half-girl actress—Sophia Evgenevna Holliday.) There, behind the door, the words were heard:
—It's me, Alya, Sonya!
I opened the door quickly, saying:
—Sophia Evgenevna!
—My dear little soul! My darling dear child! My little girl!—Holliday exclaimed.
Meantime I quickly walked up the stairs to Marina and said rapturously:
—It's Holliday!—but Marina wasn't there, because she went to the attic with Yura N.[102]
I started washing my feet. Suddenly I heard a knock on the kitchen door. I open it. Sophia Evgenevna comes in. She sits down on the chair, puts me on her lap and says:
—They left my dear child alone! I think we should tell all the guests to come here.
—But then how will I wash my feet?
—Oh, yes, that's sore.[103]
I sat with my face on the soft shoulder of Holliday. Holliday was very slightly touching my shawl. Then she left, promising to return to say goodbye. But when I saw that she wasn't coming back, I, in my nightgown with my shawl thrown on, went to her myself and climbed onto her lap. There were Yura S.,[104] one more student, and Holliday. But Marina and Yura N. had left for the attic earlier. I came bare-footed, without sandals or boots, just in my black stockings. So moving! Yura S. gave me a little white pie. Holliday was happy and petted my tangled hair. An acquaintance of Holliday's arrived. Someone's steps

---

102 Yury Sergeyevich Nikolsky (1895–1962), a composer, conductor, and music director of the Second Vakhtangov Studio.
103 Sonechka uses the St. Petersburg word instead of the Moscow word for "bad."
104 Yura S. is the actor Georgy Serov (1894–1929).

were heard on the roof. It turned out that Marina and Yura N. had gone to the roof through the attic window. Yura S. climbed onto the roof with a candle, exclaiming:

—Get me some light to save the mistress of the house!

Sitting on the windowsill, I moved slightly closer and closer to the roof. Holliday called to her acquaintance and said:

—Oh, the child is getting onto the roof! Take away this crazy child!

This girl came to take me away, but I struggled against it. Finally, Holliday herself took me and tried to carry me to my bed. I didn't struggle and said:

—Hallidah's nasty! Don't like Hallidah!

She, half-laughing, gave me to S-ov to carry, saying that I was too heavy for her arms. As soon as they put me down, I saw Marina coming from the attic. (Holliday, when she was carrying me, was saying: "Alya, calm down! you'll be the first to see Marina!") Marina held in her hand a fat candle in a brass holder. Holliday said to her:

—Marina, Alechka said that she doesn't love me!

Marina was very surprised, I think."

Second entry:

"The actress Sonechka Holliday came over. We sat in the kitchen. It was dark. She said to me:

—You know Alechka, Yura wrote a little note to me: "My dear little girl, Sonechka! I'm very glad you don't love me. I'm a very nasty person. Nobody should love me. Don't love me."

But I thought that he wrote this way on purpose, so he'd be loved more. And not despised. But I didn't tell her anything. Sonechka Holliday has a rosy pink little face and dark eyes. She's small in height and her arms are slim. I thought and thought about him all the time that he's calling this woman, so she'll love him. He's writing such notes on purpose. If he really thought that he was in truth a nasty person, he wouldn't write that."

... Not nasty. Just—weak. Passionless. With no other passions except vanity, so plentifully—so offensively—nurtured by his beauty. What do I remember from his pronouncements? My every straightforward, point-blank question about a preference, a choice of this or that—even between the Reds and the Whites, was met with, "I don't know ... It's so complicated." (Another version: "so deeply non-simple..." but in essence it meant, "I'm so indifferent.")

He was excited only by the theater. I remember once he talked to me for more than an hour about how he'd make (with his own hands?) a small theater and divide it into innumerable cages, with little people—in each, the dramatis personae of a particular play, and in the between-cages—those of a common one.

—And what kind of plays would they be? What would they all be about?

—(*He, mysteriously*) I don't know... I don't know that yet... But I see it all perfectly... (*Blissfully*) Such small ones, almost invisible.

Sometimes—he had uncertain dreams about Italy:

—Well, Pavlik and I will go to Italy. We'll walk on the Florentine hills, eat salty, braided bread, drink chianti, pick mandarins...

—(*I, echo-like*) ... and remember—Marina.

—(*He, like an echo of the echo*) And remember—Marina.

But even Italy was from Goldoni,[105] and not from the depths of heart-sickness.

Once, Pavlik said to me:

—Marina, Yura decided to stage Shakespeare.

—(*I, amusedly*) We-ell?

—Yes. *Macbeth*. And what he'll do is—not leave the half of it!

—It'd be better—if he'd add a half. Just let him—try! Maybe Shakespeare left something out? Yury Alexandrovich—found it and filled it in!

Once, after his eulogizing nonsense—you see, he grew up in the volcanic vicinity of the crazy, theatrical-to-the-bone Vakhtangov—I said to him:

—Yury Alexandrovich—hear the truth for once in your life. Women love you, but you want men to respect you.

His student friends—except Pavlik, who was in love with him, the way Pushkin was with Goncharova, except for Pavlik's lack of such beauty (the fact that Goncharova was a woman and Yury Z.—a man didn't change a thing, because Pushkin, by marrying Goncharova, didn't acquire beauty but *remained* small, quick-moving, etc.)—but Pavlik's love was also an overcoming of jealousy: it was a decision to love—something that he should essentially hate: Pavlik's love was—pure romanticism. Except for Pavlik, Yury Z-sky's student-friends treated him condescendingly—or, more exactly, they treated those of us who loved him with condescension, condescension for our

---

105   Carlo Osvaldo Goldoni (1707–1793), an Italian playwright and librettist.

weakness and our ease of seduction. —"Z-sky ... well-ell ...," and after this long *well* followed: nothing.

(Their love was mutual jealousy: Yura's of—Pavlik's gift, Pavlik's of—Yura's beauty, a jealousy which, impossible to endure, decided to turn into, and did turn into—love. And more—a secret calculation on nature's part: together they were—Lord Byron.)

Everything in Yura was—an emanation of his own beauty. But since the source (the beauty) was naturally stronger, everything else in him seemed, and proved to be, insufficient, and sometimes he, on the whole, seemed to be—unworthy of it. Nevertheless, it's a tragedy when the face is—the best thing in you, and beauty—the main thing in you, and when the commodity is—always at face value, your own face value, which at the same time is a commodity. Everyone was asking something of him in keeping with the promissory note of this beauty, theater directors—just like women. Everyone walked around him and asked for something. (I was the only one who *gave him alms* for his beauty.)—"But for goodness sake, ladies and gentlemen," he might say, "I never promised anything to anyone." No, my dear, you didn't. But such a face is already by itself—a promise. Only it promised something *you* couldn't keep. Only flowers keep such promises. And precious stones. Precious—all through. Flowery—all through. Or—Saint Sebastians. It has to be said that he wore his beauty meekly, angelically. ("Where do such things come to me from?"[106]) But this didn't improve anything, it just made things even—worse. The only way for a man—not to condescend to his own beauty is—to overlook it (overlook: look higher). But for that, one has to be—bigger, and he was—smaller. So, he himself was just as seduced by his beauty as the rest of us ...

How to describe an angel? An angel, you see, doesn't consist of anything, but is at once whole. It appears. It's apparent. When we say an angel, there's no doubt about it. We all see—the same thing.

I just add: an angel with a silver strand of hair. Twenty years old—with a gray strand of pure silver.

And, also—with a beaver-collared fur coat. A huge fur coat, because his height too was non-human: it was angelic.

Besides this non-human height, he didn't have a "figure." He, himself was—a figure. 1919 favored his "angelicism": the enormity of his fur coat or his cloak of Saint Antony, always—clothes, always—hazes. In that sense, he

---

106 Gospel of Luke 1:43.

didn't have a face either: just hollows, tints, "from field to field—the capricious wind drives the golden tints..."[107] (silver ones). There was a collective image of an angel, indubitable to such an extent that any little girl would recognize him from her dream. And—she did.

But it wasn't for nothing that an angelic image was bestowed on him, there *was* something of the angel about him: in his voice (the most inner of all our insides, it's not for nothing it's called *organe* in French), in his economical gestures, in the way he listened, with his head lowered, and how he held up his lowered head in both his hands, how he glanced—from below, how he stood like a sudden motionless apparition—in the door, and in the way he, without a trace—vanished.

His beauty, its angelic quality, taught him—something, and was still teaching him something: *it* dictated a pace to him ("he steps so carefully, as if he's afraid of smashing some little invisible creatures," as Alya put it), a gesture, an intonation. It couldn't teach him words (meanings), as if this wasn't its business—therefore he couldn't *state* anything (there was nothing!), but could *make a statement* of—everything.

That is why everyone was deceived, from a simple cleaning lady to—Sonechka and me. "He loves so much that he can't even say it..." (He didn't love *so much*—he didn't love *at all*.) "There's some sort of mystery..." There wasn't any mystery. None—except for the self-mystery of such beauty.

Beauty can teach you how to *step* (and it does!), how to *take steps*—it can't. How to *exhibit*—it can, how to *express*—it can't. The necessary voice, necessary intonation, necessary pause, necessary breathing—yes. The necessary word—no. Here we step into the other kingdom, where the kings are we—"dwarfs of the Infanta."

It's not that "there was something of the angel about him," rather—everything in him was angelic, except words and actions, word and deed. They were—very typical, half school-like, half actor-like deeds. If he was not the best of his society and his age, he was—not the worst. He was *worthless* only against the background of his beauty.

I said that in some sense he didn't have a face. But he didn't have—a guise either. He had—an appearance. There was—an appearance, namely, the angelic facade of an ordinary (and non-living) building. There was an appearance,

---

107 From a poem of Afanasy Afanasyevich Fet (1820–1892).

an image (and what I'm producing right now—a tombstone). Nevertheless, it's better that he—existed!

All this is already twenty years old—which was his age then! My poetic scatterings, *Comedian*,[108] which are also a thing of the past, were for him as he was then, about him alive then. My play *Fortuna* (in which he is Lauzun[109]) included his live cry in my room, in the freezing cold, under the dark-blue lantern of the eighteenth century:

> Is it possible that even my hands will crack?
> Damn this freezing cold!
> I pity you, my hands.

(His *damn* sounded more tender then a lute!)—I see the play of dark-blue light and light-blue shadow on his frighteningly witnessing hands... My play (a lost one) *Stone Angel*[110] is for *him*: he is the stone angel in the village square for whom the brides leave their bridegrooms, the wives—their husbands, and all lovers—their lovers. Because of him everyone drowned themselves, poisoned themselves, took the veil, but he—kept just standing there. There wasn't another act, it seems to me.[111] Good that the notebook was lost, that it too drowned itself, poisoned itself, took the veil—as they did. *His* shadow is in (and on!) my poems for Sonechka... But *he himself* is—another story. I said all this—to make Sonechka comprehensible, to show where her huge horse-chestnut-colored eyes were directed, what they were unbreakably chained to in that spring of 1919, what they were filled to the brim with, and why they always shone.

Sonechka! Let's forgive him his angelic façade!

Once I came by his place with my latest gift. I didn't catch him at home, but I did catch his nannie:

—There, you brought a little book for Yurochka to read—thank you! Let him read and enjoy himself. But there are very few, my dear, who come—with gifts. Many come, from morning to night—he hasn't opened his eyes yet—

---

108 *Comedian* is the name of the cycle of poems Tsvetaeva dedicated to Yury Z.
109 Duc de Lauzun, Marie Antoinette's lover.
110 Found and published after Tsvetaeva's death.
111 The play is in six scenes.

they call. He's just closed his eyes—they call. And mainly they come empty-handed, but with kisses. I'm not condemning these maidens—they're so young!—and Yurochka's—the best-looking of the best-looking. He was good-looking from birth. He was good-looking even carried in the arms. All maidens fell in love with him. Even I say to him: "Why are you, Yury Alexandrovich, so beautiful? It's not a male thing!"—"But Nannie, it's not my fault."—Of course, it's not his fault, but it doesn't make it any easier for me—to run and open the door... Let them kiss him! They won't kiss anything out of him, anyway. But if you're kissing him, then take care of him—bring some rice, or millet, or even a small flat cake—can't you see how skinny he is? His sister, Verochka, has been consumptive for a number of years, God forbid that he'll get sick too: they have the same face, same blood. They shouldn't bring it *to him*, of course—he won't accept it, he's a shy one—but *to me*, to the kitchen: "Here, Nannie, take this to fortify my beloved." But no, there's nothing like that! If they come to me to the kitchen—it's to cry because—he doesn't love them. They're empty-headed and empty-handed. But their mouths are full-ull: of nonsense and kisses.

But there's one who comes to see him who's—pure gold. (I have two girls who bring things—but one is so strict, like a governess, her little nose is a little too big, but I'm not talking about her now...) Do you know Miss Hallidah? She comes: "Is Yurochka home?" At first, she said Yury Alexandrovich, but then she quickly got used to me, and stopped being shy.—"He's home, my beauty," I say, "but he's asleep."—"Well, don't wake him, don't wake him. I really didn't want to come by, but here I brought something for him, but Nannie, don't tell him."

And she puts a small bag into my hands, and in it—not simply millet or rye bread, but always a white bun. A white one. Where does she get it from?!

Or she'd sit and darn socks.—"Give me, Nannie, Yurochka's socks."—"What are you thinking, miss, that's not something for your young little hands? It's for an old woman's hands."—"No!"—and she looks into my eyes earnestly, earnestly, tenderly, tenderly, "Don't call me miss, call me—Sonya and I'll call you—Nannie."—So I started to call her—Sonechka, like a little one.

And how much she loves him, I can't even tell you!

She darns his socks, irons his shirt (while he's asleep and doesn't know anything), kisses me on the cheek—"Give Yurochka my regards"—and leaves.

How many times I've said to my handsome one: "Don't think long, Yury Alexandrovich, you won't ever find better than her: she's a beauty, and a smart one, and a hard worker—acts in the theater, supports herself, and in the very darkest night will run for a doctor, raise an alarm in the whole city, but will get the doctor: one *can* get sick with such a wife! And she'll be a good mother to your children, since she took you, a beanpole, to be her son. And her height's—perfect for you: look, you're that—tall, and she's—such a little thing! (To me she says: "The lanky guys, they always like the little ones.") A zolotnik's[112] small, but it's precious.

—And he?

—Stands there, smiles, keeps silent. Doesn't love her. That's it.

—Does he love another?

—Ah, my dear, he doesn't love anyone. From birth he never loved anyone, except for his sister Verochka, and me, his Nannie.

—(I, in my thoughts: "And himself in the mirror.")

—So, to finish about Sonechka. If he isn't home, she leaves happy, but if he *is* home, she always leaves in tears. He's our chilly one.

—He is your chilly one.

A mirror is also chilly.

Sonechka also had her own nannie, Maryushka. "When I get married, I'll have my yellow chest as a dowry." She wasn't really a nannie—but an old servant, an old servant who lived in the house for a long time, as if she were—a nannie. I, during my whole friendship with Sonechka, had never seen this Maryushka—because she was always standing in lines: for herring, for vegetable oil, and for one more thing. But I constantly heard about her, as in, "Maryushka will get upset again" (about Yury, sleepless nights, millet fed to someone else . . .).

Once there was a knock on the door. I open it. A face black, due to the eyes, and right from the threshold, she says:

—Marina! Something horrible just happened. A coffin took up residence in my room.

—Wha-a-at?

—Here—listen. My Maryushka heard somewhere that coffins were being distributed—yes, real coffins (*pause*)—for the dead. Because right now,

---

[112] Zolotnik, an old Russian measure of weigh, equivalent to 4.26 grams. A Russian proverb meaning that good things come in small packages.

you know, they're—a luxury. (You know that one for Alexey Alexandrovich was made at the Studio. You'd think that they were distributed everywhere, except the Studio.) She went there—every day, every day she went there, nursing it—so that the salesmen finally lost his patience: "How soon will you die, old bag, and stop dragging yourself here for coffins? You'll die, old bag, before you get a coffin"—and similar sorts of courtesies. But she's a tough one: "Since it was promised, it's promised. I won't give up mine." And walks there, and walks there.

And finally, she goes today and—there it is! Yes, yes, in exchange for thirty ration coupons: "So, old bag, is this the happiness you've been waiting for?"—And he puts in front of her, in the middle of the counter, a blue coffin: "Well, try it on and see if you'll fit in it with all your bones?"—"I'll fit,' she says, "but not in that one."—"How do you mean not in this one?"—So, she says, "This one's blue, a male one, but I'm a maiden and supposed to have a pink one. So, if you, please, be so kind and give me a little pink one, because the blue one I won't take, not for anything in the world."—"Wha-a-at are saying," he says, "you old crone? It's not enough that you've spoiled so much of my blood. In addition, you've turned out to be a *maiden* who'd like to luxuriate in a pink one! You won't get a pink one, you devilish old bag, because we don't have them in our factory."—

"'Then, your honor, maybe I can get me a white one,'—I say to him, very scared that he will send me away without my little coffin, because to lie in a male coffin is—a dishonor for a maiden, and I, from my very first swaddling clothes to my shroud, am an honorable one. Here he started—stamping his foot at me: 'Take what you're given, you devilish maiden—and get out, otherwise I'll make a misfortune! Now,' he screams, 'is a revolutionary time, a time of great distress. It doesn't discriminate between men and women, especially—corpses . . . So, take it, take it now, otherwise I'll coffin you with it!'—and he raised the coffin lid at me! Shame, embarrassment, the soldiers around roaring with laughter, pointing their fingers at me . . . Well, I see that there's nothing to be done, so I load my eternal rest on my back and go home. And I was so bitter, miss, how long I was dragging myself there for it, how many jokes I had to endure, but it looks like I'll have to find repose in a male one, a blue one."—

And now, Marina, it's in my room. Have you seen the deep shelf above my door—the one for suitcases? She begged me to put it there: so that it won't be under anyone's feet, and, the main thing—so it won't wound her eyes with the color. "Because as soon as I look at it, miss, the grievance is spilled all over me."

So, there it stands. (*Pause.*)—Perhaps I'll get used to it, someday.

(This was Ascension Day, 1919.)

So *the fourth* character in Sonechka's room was—a coffin.

And here is my Sonechka, seen by different eyes: those of a stranger:

—I saw your Sonechka Holliday today. I was riding on a tram and I saw her—standing, holding onto the leather strap, reading something, smiling. Then suddenly on her shoulder appeared a huge paw, a soldier's one. And you know what she did? Without stopping reading and even without stopping smiling, she calmly took this paw away from her shoulder—like a thing.

—That's the living image of—her! Are you sure it was—her?

—Oh, yes. You see, I went to see her in *White Nights* many times. She was the same, in the white dress, with two braids. It was so . . . chaar-ming (*my interlocutor was from the Kingdom of Poland*) that the whole carriage laughed and one even screamed: bravo!

—And what did she do?

—Nothing. She didn't even raise her eyes. Only, maybe her smile—became a bit wider . . . She's so adorable.

—You find her so?

—With her downcast eyes and with these braids, she's—a real Madonna. She probably has many love affairs.

—No. She loves only children.

—Well . . . But that *doesn't* . . .

—Yes, it does interfere.

This is how I protected Sonechka from the paws of the bourgeoisie.

Love affairs?

"I never knew exactly what kind of relations she had with men, whether they were what one might call liaisons, or something else. But whether you dream together or sleep together you always cry in solitude."[113]

---

113   *Je n'ai jamais su au juste ce qu' étaient ses relations avec les hommes, si c' étaient ce qu' on appelle des liaisons—ou d' autres liens. Mais rêver ensemble ou dormir ensemble, c' était toujours pleurer seule.* Perhaps a quotation from an unknown source.

II

Volodya[1]

Word one: his appearance—well-built, and—right away, before one's eyes, stands—his torso, an inverted triangle, where everything is given to the shoulders, and nothing—to the waist.

A first impression of his face—the letter T, and even a complete cross: with a vertical wrinkle cleaving through the eyebrows and continuous with the straightness of his nose.

But here—I stop, because the rest of the visual impression is—*word two*.

He had a deep voice that came from out of the depths, and therefore resonated in the deep.

And it was—deeply fascinating, deep, and deeply fascinating.

But—not melodic. There was nothing of the instrument, everything of the human voice in the full measure of its humanity and vocal cords.

Everything in him, from head to toe, said: *Voilà un homme!*[2]

Even the extreme youth in him was yielding to this *homme*. Only later did people guess that he was young—very young.

In him, by replacing the Consul—with the young man, and the Emperor with—the man, you had made real in front of your eyes Hugo's couplet:

> And ever was the First Consul's tight mask
> Pierced by the forehead of the Emperor.[3]

The man in him came through equally and everywhere in front of your eyes. This young man was wearing his future face.

From Pavlik A., I'd already been hearing daily for the entire year about this Volodya—with the constant addition of—"remarkable." "There's such

---

1   Vladimir Vasilyevich Alekseev (1892–1919), an actor.
2   There's a man!
3   *Et du Premier Consul déjà en maint endroit*
      Le front de l'Empereur perçait le masque étroit.
   From "This century has ten years . . .," in *Autumn Leaves*.

a remarkable person in our Studio—Volodya." But he didn't bring *this* friend to me.

Our first encounter was—during the winter of 1918–19, on the cold downhill of 1918, at the party of a merry lady, who was trying to look younger than her age, who raised her leg as if it were her arm, and with her leg-arm greeted art—all art, including mine and me. There were many such ladies during the revolution at its beginning, who at the end of the old world celebrated the end of their youth. At its beginning. By 1919 they'd all left.

His first words in this deep voice were:

—But kings do not just submit to traditions, they create them.

His first words—to me, at the end of the party, during which we said not a single word to each other (he sat and watched people playing cards, I didn't even do that) were:

—You remind me of George Sand.[4] She also had children, *also* wrote, and had a hard life on Majorca, when the stove wouldn't light.[5]

I invited him over immediately. He came the next morning—we went for a walk. He was hungry. We shared and ate my piece of bread right on the street.

Later he said:

—I liked everything immediately, everything. That you invited me without knowing me. That you said, tomorrow. Women normally don't do that: it's always the day after tomorrow, as if tomorrow they're always very busy. That we didn't stay at home but—went for a walk. And that you broke the bread in half and ate it too. I felt—a ritual in that.

And then, even later:

—At Zoya Borisovna's[6] you reminded me of a young Polish lady: you had on a sort of (*helplessly*), a sort of little jacket perhaps? Velvety-smoky with fur trimming. In short—a *kontusz*[7]? And the set of your head was slightly thrown back. And your glance—slightly from above. I right away sensed—Polish blood in you.

---

4   A French novelist and memoirist (1804–1876).
5   Described in *A Winter in Majorca* (1841), an autobiographical travel novel written at the time of Sand's relationship with Frederic Chopin, not fully published until 1942.
6   The woman at whose party they met.
7   A traditional Polish coat.

He started coming over. He started coming often—twice a week, right after the performance, that is, after twelve. We sat in the opposite corners of the rusty-colored couch, or better: he sat in its deep corner, I across on the shallow outer edge. Our conversation took place on a long diagonal, the longest path from one to the other.

He was dark. Very big eyes, dark from their lashes, but themselves—gray. His whole face was linear, without even a small curve, chiseled. In his face the same straight-forwardness as in his body. It was *la tête de son corps*.[8] As if this face was part of—his torso. (The only thing that wasn't straight in this whole appearance was—his side parting, which, naturally, was straighter than a straight one.)

Visual—straightness, inner—straightforwardness. Of the voice, of the movement, of the look in the eyes, of the handshake. Everything had—one meaning and, along the shortest straight line between two dots, stood: him—and the world.

Straightforwardness—and firmness. Or even—inexorability. And, along with utter openness—impenetrability, not in the sense of inner enigma or mystery, but in the simplest way: the material from which he was made. Such material a hand doesn't touch, and if it does—it touches nothing except the hand itself, and has no effect. So, it's useless to touch. Just like with a statue, he was tangible, accessible, but—impenetrable. In some sense—a thing without resonance.

In a word—the furthest thing from a portrait. Despite his nonexistent plasticity, but perhaps because of it, he was endlessly reachable and complaisant, as if with a frame that could be peered a mile into at will, or, from within all of its hundred years—looked out from into a room. He was the very opposite of a portrait. He was like a statue, with its edgy appearance, its extremely edgy appearance, that sets obstacles to the eyes at every point of its surface.

("Is that really me, Marina Ivanovna?"—"Yes, it's all you—Volodechka. But it's too early to be upset—wait a little.")

(As it emerged later—this impression of his statuesqueness was mistaken. But that was—later, when I'd already fed on this error for a year-and-a-half, and for a year-and-a-half was building on it—and built on it.)

Immediately, he became—a friend. Immediately, the only friend—and a stronghold.

---

8 The head that went with his body.

In Moscow of 1918–19, I—so steadfast in myself, so straightforward and steely in myself—couldn't share him with anyone. In Moscow of 1918–19, out of my circle of young men—to tell you the truth—only trash was left. Utter "students," hiding from the war in those newly opened studios . . . and in their talents. Or Red youth, on leave between two battles, perhaps beautiful, but I couldn't be friends with them. For there could be no friendship between the victor and the vanquished.

With Volodya, I unburdened my male soul.

I immediately started calling him Volodechka, out of great gratitude that he wasn't in love, that I wasn't in love, and that everything was so amicable: trusting.

And he called me—Maria Ivanovna, never deviating from it, and even saying a final goodbye in this name-and-patronymic way. I was very grateful to him for this, since everyone else called me plain Marina. Nobody called me Maria Ivanovna! By this patronymic, he immediately separated himself—from them. And, in his own way—appropriated me.

Our conversations? About stars: once, when returning from someone, we stayed for an hour in my lane—up to the knees in snow, talking about the stars. I remember a raised hand, which was raised higher and higher, and the name Flammarion[9]—and *Flammarion* eyes—looking into mine, only to raise mine to the stars. The snow pile was growing: there wasn't a snowstorm, since there were stars, but the snow pile, from our long standing there, was growing—or were we sinking into it? One more hour of standing and—it would have been a snow house and we'd have been inside it.

What else did we talk about? About Joan of Arc—the miracle of her appearance, about Napoleon on Saint Helena—about Jack London, then his favorite writer—never about the theater.

And—never about poems. There were never any poems—from me to him. None read, none written. What I had with him was deeper than love, deeper than poems. Something we both—needed more. And it must have been—the most needed thing in the world, more needed than my need of him and his of me.

About his life (his loves, family) I knew nothing. I never asked. He came from the darkness of the winter night, which became even darker during the

---

9   Nicolas Camille Flammarion (1842–1925), a French astronomer and author.

hours and hours of our sitting together—he left in it too. ("Into the lighter night," will come later.)

And even in my thoughts I never saw him off. Volodya ended behind the door and started there too. That interval was—his life.

Hand on my heart: I don't remember if we ever said: "When are you coming?" etc. But there wasn't a time—during that winter that he came and I wasn't home, and there wasn't a time when someone else was there when he came. Yet of "set days" we had none. Sometimes he came twice a week and sometimes once in two weeks: "So, are you always at home and always on your own?"—"No, I was out."—"No, people came by." But that was our miracle and there wasn't a time when I, at the sight of him, didn't exclaim: "Volodya! I was just thinking about you!" Or: "Volodya, if you only knew how much I was dreaming you'd come today!" Or simply; "Volodya! What happiness!"

Because happiness came in with him—for the whole evening, reliable, faithful happiness, like a favorite book for which one doesn't really need light.

Happiness without a fear of tomorrow: what if he stops loving me? doesn't come anymore? etc. Happiness without a tomorrow and without the expectation of it: without having to walk the streets with large steps—stand on icy feet during icy nights,—look in the window...

I'll tell you more: I never missed him, and, as reliably as I didn't miss him, I was happy to see him. I dreamt about him—yes, but as calmly as I did about a thing that I certainly will have, as about a registered letter that I already know—was sent. (When it will arrive is—the post office's business, not mine.)

He always sat there—without his fur coat. Despite the cold, even freezing cold, he was—always without it. In his gray suit, as elegant as his figure, which looked as stately as he himself—all silhouette, all—delimited from the surrounding things and walls. He more often sat straight, but if leaning—never sprawling, as if there wasn't a wall behind his back, but—a cliff. A marine landscape invariably appeared behind him and when I saw him (only once!) on stage, in a play with a nautical theme—either *The Ruins of Hope*[10] or

---

10   Probably the Dutch play *Putting Our Fate in the Hands of God* (1890), by Herman Heijermans (1864–1924).

A Flood[11]—I didn't feel any distance from my Volodya, but the opposite—maybe, for the first time, I saw him in his real place, a marine and male one.

I'd been hearing from Pavlik throughout the whole year: "Volodya's a good-looker . . . Not, of course, in the *same way* Yura is, that is, just as good-looking, but not in the *same way*. Do you understand me?"—"Oh, yes! Because Yura could easily be a female beauty, but Volodya—no way . . ."

That's why I met with Volodya's good looks for the first time on my threshold as something given and never thought about again, that is, I acted toward it in same way as he did—from birth. Since it didn't bother him, it didn't bother me. It didn't embarrass or fill him up. In the same way it didn't embarrass me or fill me up. His good looks didn't stand between us—or sit like an annoying child that always has to be paid attention to, pacified, otherwise he might burn down the whole house from boredom.

Let me say from the outset that there was no third thing between us, there was a couch-long vocal pathway from one to the other, slightly shorter than from one star to another, and there was a person (I) in front of the perfect apparition of a statue. Maybe, I even sat far away from him to see better and let this statue better situate itself, creating a perspective that way, which I was deprived of internally with him. And by creating such a physical perspective in place of the other, the internal one, which people call the future, and which, between a man and a woman, is—love.

Once I asked him jokingly:

—Volodechka, don't you, with your good looks, get sick of women, of women clinging to you?

With an embarrassed smile, in a straightforward voice, he replied:

—Marina Ivanova, they cling to every young man. Especially to an actor. If you're afraid of the wolves[12] . . . But I feel pity for them, for all women. Es-. pecially—the not such young ones. Because all of us are immeasurably guilty before them. In everything.

—And you?

---

11   Tsvetaeva seems to be correct in this second guess, as we can see from the history of the performances of the Second Studio, which staged *A Sin Flood* by Swedish writer Johan Henning Berger (1872–1924).

12   A Russian saying: "If you're afraid of the wolves, don't go into the forest."

—I (*with an earnest look*), I am trying—to correct it.

Besides me, he was also friendly with another student—with a Caucasus last name. When he praised her too much, I was jokingly jealous and slightly made fun of her, though I'd never seen her. And every time he said:

—No, no, Marina Ivanovna, you shouldn't be laughing. Even jokingly. Because she's a remarkable human being. (*He was non-yielding, like a cliff.*) She was a sister of mercy during the war (*in a tone of highest recognition*)—she was in the war.

—But I—wasn't.

—You—didn't need to be, you've got—a different thing.

—To sit and write poems? Oh, I'm actually insulted!

—No, not to sit and write poems, but to do what you do.

—And what do I do?

—This, what you do—with me, and—all that you will yet do with me.

—Volodya, don't.

—I *won't*.

Once he brought her to me. And—oh, joy!—this young woman was not beautiful. Clearly, non-beautiful. She was as clearly non-beautiful as he was—handsome. And this non-beautiful one, he who was—spoiled (if he was) and loved (if he was) by many—preferred to everyone. With *her* he passed the time—that he didn't pass with me.

An attempt to—correct?

Volodya came to me with stories—like presents that were substantial enough to be carried in the hand and delivered to my house—precisely to my house, and he placed them in my heart—as if in my hand.

I remember one of his stories, about a French pilot who was killed in the war. A crashed machine, a killed man. And then, after some time—the victorious bird returns—descends, and disregarding the enemy territory, the German victor—throws a wreath to—the Frenchman he'd shot down.

With such stories he fed and watered me during those long nights.

They were never—about the theater, except once, when he said laughingly:

—Marina Ivanovna, you won't suspect me of vanity, will you?

—No.

—Because it was very well said. You'll—appreciate it. We have a cleaning lady at the Studio, a lovely young girl, and everyone mocks me about her—

saying that she's in love with me. It's nonsense, of course. I simply chat with her and joke—she's young, you see, and could easily be my stage partner and not a cleaning lady. Among women, you see, high birth and social class play a much smaller role. They have two social classes: youth and old age. Isn't that so? Well, she said to me today—as I was wiping off my make-up, cleaning my face: "Ah, Volodechka Alexeyev you're such a cruel good-looker!"—"What are you saying Dunya?" I reply. "How am I a cruel good-looker? It's our Z-sky who's a cruel good-looker."—"No," she says, "Yury Alexandrovich's beauty is angelic, city beauty, and you, Volodechka, have a marine, military one. That real, unbearably cruel, male beauty, the heroic one. In our village everyone would laugh at Yury Alexandrovich, but for you, Volodechka, the three villages would lose their mind." That's the sort of hero (*pensively*) I am . . .

—"Beauty may be terrifying . . ."[13] And now, Volodya, in keeping with your cruel good-looker, I'll tell you my story:

From my birth I remember Maria Vasilevna in our house. Who exactly she was, I don't know, she must have been—a maid of *all* work. If one of the children got sick, if the clothes' chest needed airing, or something needed to be re-sewn, or eggs needed painting—she took care of it. And then she disappeared. She was skinny—almost a skeleton, but had marvelous, marvelous eyes, full of suffering, live suffering. They were dark-brown—not black (only Asians or, very silly people have black ones, like beads)—and they were as big as her face, which was scarcely visible. Even though she was old, she was not really old—not even one gray hair, but black or blue-black hair with a middle parting. Well, she was like—a nun, or even better—an old Mother of God with her son. And that's how it was: she had a son—I was very small at the time—Sasha, who was a student in trade school. He lived in our annex, near the kitchen. Then, when we were abroad with mother, he became consumptive, and my father sent him to Sukhumi.[14]—"Ah, Musen'ka,[15] how he was waiting for me, how much he was waiting! He was so close to dying, and was waiting for me with every passing ship. When a ship would blow, he'd say: 'That's my mother coming to me!' (The nurse told me afterwards.) And I truly was on my way to him—your father gave me the money, and the yard caretaker bought a ticket for me at the train station and put me on the train—it was my first time

---

13   A slightly changed line from Alexander Blok's poem, "Beauty is terrifying, one hears."
14   Sokhumi or Sukhumi, a city on the Black Sea coast.
15   One of Marina's childhood pet names.

going so far. So, I'm on my way and he's waiting for me. And when it was about time for us to land, the ship blew its horn. And he—raised himself on his bed, stretched his arms, said, 'Mama came!'—and fell down, dead...'

...I'm telling you all this to give you a picture of her face, because she had the same face even when she was making semolina porridge, or talking about the wife of the general's pugs—always that same face. And now about this cruel beauty—here's another story, from her youth.—"I, Musen'ka—don't look at me now that I'm a relic, yellower than a lemon and my teeth loose—I, Musen'ka, was a beauty. And I was fifteen years old. I go to buy something at a shop. A young fellow follows me in. I walk out—and so does he. I walk home, look out of the window—and there he stands, looking at the curtain. In appearance, he's—dark-haired, huge eyes—no mustache yet, maybe sixteen or so. And, as God is my witness, he looks like me, he has—the same eyes. You see, about my eyes they deafened my ears, singing their praises, so I knew well—what my eyes looked like on my face. I look at him—and there are *my* eyes, my own. In word—a brother. (But I was an only child.) Simply put—to tell takes time, but to look is—quick. So I pull the curtain at once.

"The next day I go to the shop again, and he's already standing there, waiting. He says nothing, doesn't bow, only looks. And from that day it goes on: he follows me like a shadow and stands like—a stump. Well, on the fifth day maybe—my heart couldn't handle it anymore: I was annoyed at his looking, annoyed at his silence. So, as he follows me out of the shop, I say—to him: 'There's nothing to look at and nothing to stand for, because you won't get anything, because I'm engaged. I'm getting married: to a rich man.'

"And he, it was spring, stands under the little trees, takes off his cap and bows low to me. And suddenly—turns pale as wax. Next day—I'm still asleep—there are screams, noise: a young fellow has cut his throat at the Yegorov's. Probably at night—he's cold already. Everyone runs there—and so do I.

"Lying there, Musen'ka, my not-that-long-ago acquaintance, the starer, only the eyes, *my* eyes, wouldn't be seeing anymore: they were closed."

...And so Volodechka, what about your cleaning lady?

—No, Marina Ivanovna, the times are different now, everything has become awfully cheap. And I'd... feel it if—if she'd truly... No, she'll get married—and have children.

—And the oldest one will be called—Volodechka.

—*Possibly.*

With such stories I fed and watered him on the long nights: he—on the deep corner of the couch, I on its shallow corner, under the blue lantern, along the diagonal—which represented our whole path from one to the other, and which led us nowhere.

. . . Now, I think (and even knew then!) that—Volodya was—a traveling companion and that the path wasn't from one to the other but—away—a common road from within ourselves. And from this came the spaciousness, calmness, reliability—and unhurriedness: there is hurry only to that eternal dead end, from which there is only one way, the way back, step by step, taking away all that was given, even stamping on it, even trampling it down, with a foot like a shovel, leveling it.

Volodya of course knew about my enchantment—there's no other word for it—with Yury Z. But he never touched it, or maybe it didn't touch him. Only when I, worn out by the long disappearance of Yury Z. (and he started to disappear early—right away really!), asked in the most indifferent voice, "And how is Z-sky?" did he respond. "Z-sky's okay. Acting."

Z-sky was the only thing on which he indulged me. Z-sky's name, uttered by me, right away put Volodya in a tower and me—in a small garden beneath it, in its very rose bush. And how good it was. Suddenly, my general superiority (which with him was—an equality) was diminished, like a little girl staring from her rosy pinkness up at the stone angel. For Volodya, for whom I was always on the top of a tower—was a tower myself—it was somehow awkward to see me being younger (silly). Even while answering questions about Yury Z., he didn't physically raise his eyes—so that I was talking to his downcast eyelids.

Once, I burst out:

—Volodya, do you despise me very much for this?

He—as if he had fallen from the sky—replied:

—I—despise—you? How is it possible to despise—the sky above my head! But to end this once and for all: there are things that a man can't ever understand in a woman. Even—I, even—in you. Not because it's above and beyond our understanding. That's *not* the point. But because some things one can understand only from the inside, by being. I can't be a woman. And so this small exclusively male something in me can't understand that small exclusively female something in you. My one-thousandth part—your one-thousandth part, the one part in you that any woman could understand, any woman, even if she understands *nothing* else in you. Z-sky is—your mutual female secret... (*grinning*)—even plot.

Without understanding, I accept it, as I always accept everything in you—and from you—because you are for me beyond judgment.

—Is he a good actor?

—For his own roles. That is, where he doesn't have to *be*, but only to appear, emerge, walk, pronounce. See, I'm saying it to you honestly, without over- or under-stating it. But it's not the actor in him that you...

—And you know, Volodechka, you, who knows everything—that I'd give up the whole of Z-sky, and all my poems to him, and my whole self with him, and am giving it up, for an hour of conversation with you—this way. You on that end and I on the other...

He's silent.

... And if I had a choice, all of him versus all of our nothing-at-all... In a word, do you know that you, with only one handshake, make him vanish from my soul as if by sleight of hand?

He's still silent.

—That I... you endlessly more?!

—I know that, Marina Ivanovna.

Long, long days...[16]

No—not that, but:

Long, long nights....

When did he leave? Not at sunrise, because in the winter the sun rises late, but basically of course—in the morning: maybe four or five? Where did he go? To what life? (Without me.) Did he love anyone, as I did—Z-sky? Was he healing himself with me from some unhappy, indecent love? I don't know and will never know.

---

16 Possibly a quote from the poem "To our mother, Love" by Mikhail Alekseevich Kuzmin (1872–1936), Russian poet, musician, and novelist.

I've never met in such a young person—so great a passion for justice. (Not *his*—for justice, but justice's—passion in him.) Because he was a very, very old twenty years: "Why should I get a ration, just because—I'm an actor, and he isn't? That's unjust." This was his main argument, a reason for his whole existence, as if justice (being *exactly* what it is!) were something completely univocal, and, in all cases—indubitable, obvious, tangible, substantial, always visible right away to the naked eye from anywhere—like the old onion-dome of the Cathedral of Christ the Savior from the darkest alley of Neskuchny.[17]

Unjust—full stop. And that's that. And there's already no temptation. Unjust meant—*no*. And this wasn't simply head, it was backbone. That's why Volodya held himself so straight—his backbone was justice.

He said *not just* in the same way that Prince S. M. Wolkonsky[18] said—*unseemly*. A different generation—a different vocabulary, but it was—the same thing. Oh, how I recognize the incontrovertibility of his main argument! As the poor say: *too expensive*, and the dealer says—*impractical*—that's how Volodya said: that's not just. His "*not* just" was: *unrighteous*.

Volodya, like all in this Studio, was a student of Stakhovich[19]—but not in the same way as other students:

—Marina Ivanovna, Stakhovich teaches us the results—of centuries. But I think the point is not how it's supposed to be—how to bow, but rather—why bow this way, how, from the first savage, we came to—such a bow. From tearing one another with our teeth, for example—to dueling. This Stakhovich doesn't teach us. (*with a grin*) On his view, we have no time now—for the *history* of gesture, we need . . . the gesture, the direct benefit, and the instant result: you walk in and you bow, like Stakhovich, you walk out and you fight, like Stakhovich. But this other thing I learn myself, I go over his lessons—backwards, to the source, and you know how difficult it is to establish what the source of the Rhine or of a tribe is . . . For me his bow and his *bon ton* aren't—an answer, but a question, a question of modernity—put to the past, my

---

17 Neskuchny Garden, the oldest park in Moscow.

18 Prince Serge Wolkonsky (1860–1937), one of the first Russian proponents of eurhythmics and a friend of Tsvetaeva.

19 Tsvetaeva's diary (February/March 1919) has an autobiographical entry entitled "The Death of Stakhovich."

question—to these, and I try to find out the answer myself, because I, Marina Ivanovna (*thoughtfully*), I . . . don't know whether Stakhovich himself could answer it. Stakhovich was given all these bows at his birth, this was his gift from his ancestors—to his cradle. I have no such ancestors, Marina Ivanovna, and nobody put anything in my cradle. I came into this world—naked. But even though I'm naked, I shouldn't meaninglessly put on someone else's ever-so-beautiful dress. It's their business to bring it to me and mine—to comprehend it.

And I already understood much, Marina Ivanovna, and will tell you that it is least of all—form, and most of all—essence. Stakhovich teaches us to *be*. His lessons are—lessons in being. Because—excuse my rough example—you cannot, after bowing this way, strike each other on the jaw. You can't even say such words, or even think them, and if you can't think them—you are already a different person. That is how this bow is already inside me.

After the death of Stakhovich he told me:

—I'm very obliged to him. Because sometimes, Marina Ivanovna, since I'm young and now there is the Revolution, I'm often surrounded by rough people—and when I'm tempted to respond in their way, to speak their own language—even with a fist—the thought immediately comes to my mind: this isn't—Stakhovich-like. And—my tongue doesn't work. And—my arm doesn't raise. It will raise, Marina Ivanovna, but at the right hour—and never as a fist!

At Stakhovich's funeral:

> By the desert of Devichye Polye[20]
> Behind a coffin plunging treading
> Snow piling—pot holes—snow piling
> Moscow: nineteen-nineteen.

I, among his other young escorts, especially remember Volodya, the particular straightness of his torso under the blows of the coffin and above the snow piles, not even one step behind his teacher. The oldest and favorite grandson would have walked that way.

And—what is that? What is that? Above a small crystal-clear cross, a rosy pink face, striking in its purity and joy—with black eyes, as if embracing

---

20   Maidens' Field, a historical medical school in the Khamovniki District of Moscow. The lines are Tsvetaeva's.

the cross with her two black braids—was Sonechka at Scriabin's neighboring grave.[21] That was my first vision of her after the one on the stage, at the reading of *Snowstorm*, my first meeting with her after my *Snowstorm*, in another snowstorm, wailing and raging at the open grave, into which this grand, durable, made-at-the-Art-Theater, and too wide *coffin*—didn't fit. The frowning students were widening the hole, striking the frozen ground with shovels, wearing their shovels away on it, as if fighting it to the death—with their shovels. The girl was kneeling among the piles of snow, embracing with her arms and entangling the neighboring crystal cross with her braids, flooding it with her tears, and lighting it up with her eyes and cheeks in such way that the cross was ablaze and shining—in this perfect, sunless, snowstorm.

—How I wanted, after this whole torment, Marina—do you remember that horrid cry: "Father, hurry up, another deceased is by the gates!"—as if the deceased *himself* had come and stood with his own coffin on his shoulders, as if he was carrying it, Marina!—Marina, how I wanted, ached, *howled*—to go home with you, and warm up from this whole death business. It didn't matter which "home"—any home where I'd be alone with you, and put my head on your lap—like it is now—and I'd tell you all about Yura, and give him to you right away, if only you'd take my head in your hands and stroke it gently, and tell me that not everyone had died yet, and that I hadn't died—like all of them. Oh, how I envied Vakhtang Levanovich, who was walking with you and linking arms, and once even—put his arm around your shoulder. During this long way—he walked with you alone, with your brown fur-coat, which you sometimes, because of the wind, almost wrapped him in, so he'd think that *you* were—his, and that he was walking with you under one coat, and that you—loved him! Afterwards I said to him: "Vakhtang Levanovich, how could you not call me to walk with you! You are a bad friend."—"But, Sophia Evgenevna, I was walking with Marina Ivanovna."—"That's precisely what I'm talking about—you were walking with Marina Ivanovna!"—"But . . . I didn't know, Sophia Evgenevna. How could I know that you'd suddenly want to walk with me!"—"Not with you, you savage, but with her: *you* were walking with her and not *I*!" He, Marina, was very insulted and called me a comedienne and something else . . . But I, you see, said it—from the fullness of my heart. But

---

21 A. Scriabin (1872–1915), a Russian composer and pianist. Tsvetaeva, as we see from her journals of 1918–1919, was a friend of his second wife. The cross, now stolen, marked his grave.

now (*blissfully squinting her eyes from below*)—two months later—maybe even to the day, *I am with you*, and not just walking outside, but the way it is now, looking up at you with my eyes, hugging you with my arms, and it's warm and not cold, and we don't need to go anywhere, where we'll have to say goodbye, because I have already come, we've already come here, and I won't be going anywhere away from you Marina—ever.

There is no Novodevichye Cemetery anymore. That whole suburb is gone. Now it's a city center. The crystal cross, I've no doubt, stands and shines in a different cemetery, but what has happened to its neighbor, the simple oak cross?

Volodya, just like me, loved everything old. And in the same way he shocked each of his circles by the novelty of his opinions, but always putting this novelty somehow in parentheses—in smirk quotes. Old—but in a young way. Old—but not decrepit. This was enough not to be understood by zealots of either the old or the new world. Old—but interpreted in his own way. Past—but in a never-yet-used way. Another reason why he felt so good with me, even during our first meeting at the unduly arm-and-leg lady's, was that I noticed on his hand a big, old-fashioned, silver ring—a signet. Later I asked him: "Where is it from? Is it yours, that is, . . ."—"No, Marina Ivanovna, it's *not* a family ring. I bought it by chance, because my initials V. A. were on it. (*Pause.*) You know, Z-sky polishes his with chalk. And he doesn't know what's written on it, because it's Chinese. Don't you find that chalking is somehow chalk talking?[22] I don't polish *mine* with chalk. I like it when silver darkens. Let it be dark, like its origins."

("But Z-sky polishes his," that is—*mine*, and this Volodya—knew. That chalk right away turned into a nine-line poem:

> In an armchair lazy feeling
> I am stationed nearby kneeling—
> Waiting just to do your bidding.
>
> From the sleepy chair a hand is hanging.
> Without a sound it's in my keeping,

---

22   A play on words. *Mel* means chalk, *melko* means shallow. The whole phrase means, "Chalking the ring is sort of shallow."

> A signet ring with Chinese writing,
>
> The signet polished up with chalking.
> Are you happy? Not my planning.
> It was what my love was bidding.[23]

This "not my planning" I afterward, in the hand-written notebook of my poems to him, which I gave him as a present, changed to "not my tiding.")

I gave Yury Z. the silver Chinese one and Pavlik A. the German cast-iron one with gold, which probably came from some captive or killed person. It had cast-iron roses on its inner gold rim, with gold concealed, underneath. Along with it, I gave him a poem:

> I'm giving you this ring of iron:
> Insomnia—rapture—and despair,
> So you'll not look at women's faces,
> So you'll forget the name for—love.
>
> So you'll lift up your crazy curls
> Like a foamy goblet in the air.
> So you'll to ashes—dust—and earth—
> Be turned by this iron ornament.
>
> When into your prophetic curls
> Love itself will enter ember-like,
> Then be quiet and press your lips
> To the iron ring on your dark finger.
>
> Here's a talisman from my red lips
> Here's a first link for your shirt of mail—
> So in the storm of days you'll stand oak-like,
> Alone, like a god, in this iron ring.[24]
>
> (Moscow, March, 1919)

I don't know the fate of the Chinese ring (I know only one thing: I gave him a ring first!), but the fate of the iron one is as follows:

---

23 From Tsvetaeva's cycle of poems *Comedian*, inspired and dedicated to Zavadsky.
24 Also from Tsvetaeva's *Comedian*.

Time went by. One day Pavlik came by—no ring. "Did you lose it?"—"No, I gave it to be cut, so as to make *two*. (*I thought: Pavlik, it'll be less!*) Two wedding ones. Because I'm getting married, to Natasha."—"Well, the best of luck to you! And the poems, did you also cut them in two?"

After that—we saw one another rarely—again, no ring.—"Where's the ring, Pavlik, I mean the half-ring?"—"Marina Ivanovna, it was a disaster! When we made it into two—they both turned out to be so thin that Natasha's golden one broke right away, and when I went to the basement for the coal, mine rolled somewhere there and since it was also black..."—"So it has probably already been burnt up in the stove for a family soup. Such luxury—to boil millet on a war prisoner's iron roses, given by *me*!"

The fate of Volodya's—own—ring lies ahead. Besides the ring, Volodya also had one other antique thing, a pistol—the "Gispanish pishtol," as we called it. And this pistol, I, out of my love for him, put into my play *Adventure* and gave it to my (Casanova's[25]) Henrietta:

> Ah, do not forget the Gispanish pishtol,
> your present!

He brought this "pishtol" at New Year's and solemnly handed to me—because he, like me, couldn't stand to keep something that someone else had a passionate liking for.

I had to leave it in Russia, burying it together with someone's Maltese sword—about which I'm going to be talking in the future. To be more exact—its body was left in Russia, but in *Adventure* I took its soul across a frontier—of time and visibility.

For this New Year I wrote a poem for all three of them:[26]

> Dear friends! Blood-brothers three in one.
> Closer, though, than blood!
> Dear friends in Soviet—Jacobean—
> Marat's Moscow town![27]

---

25 Giacomo Casanova (1725–1798).

26 From *Comedian*.

27 Jean-Paul Marat (1743–1793), a French political theorist, physician, and scientist, best known for his role as a radical journalist and politician during the French Revolution.

> I'll start with you, fervent A-sky,[28]
> Favorite of the frigid Muses,
> Remembering only that after
> A Polish panna I am named.
>
> Hence your fraternal coldness
> And a web of other obstacles!—
> Remembering not even that: Z-sky!
> Yourself most memorable.
>
> And finally—the hero of the maskers—
> Coming from the words *to be*[29]
> By whom all names are forgotten
> Including his! by—Aleks-v![30]
>
> And, exercising this ancient art
> Of hiding like a diamond in the rough,
> I listen with tenderness and sadness,
> Like the ancient Sibyl[31]—and George Sand!

That was when Volodya brought me his "pishtol" as a present, on January 1, 1919.

As a present for the New Year of 1919, which I celebrated with them, I gave—to the whole Third Studio—my ancient silver mask of a Greek king, one from an archeological excavation. A masque is—always a tragedy, but the mask of a king is—tragedy itself. I remember—it was at the theater—their grateful *Fackelzug*,[32] arranged by the students for Bettina.[33]

> ... Like the ancient Sibyl—and George Sand ...

Yes, yes, I felt that all of them, who were barely younger than I, or my own age, were—my sons, because I was long married and had two children, and two books of poems—and so many notebooks of poems!—and so many

---

28 Pavlik Antokolsky.
29 "Stakhovich teaches us to *be*." See p. 78.
30 Volodya.
31 In ancient Greece, the sibyls were women with oracular powers.
32 A torchlight procession.
33 Bettina von Arnim (the Countess of Arnim) (1785–1859), a German writer, novelist, publisher, composer, singer, visual artist, patron of young talent, and social activist.

abandoned countries! But it is not just my marriage, my children, my notebooks, not even my counties—I started *remembering* everything from the time when I started living, and to remember—is to age. And I, despite my fountain of youth, was old, old as a mountain cliff that didn't remember when it started.

They, you see, were children—and actors (that is, double children), with one sole dream of something that I had so easily and unwantedly attained, something that just came by itself—a name.

—Oh, how I'd like fame! So, when walking there'd be whispering behind my back: "There goes A-sky!"

—But it's just *girls* whispering, Pavlik! Is that really—flattering? In your place, I'd suddenly turn and walk up to them like dogs, and say: "Yes, A-sky! and so?"

All of them, except Volodya, I wholly—flattered.

I loved them. That makes a difference.

I didn't have an animal-like (mother-like) tenderness toward Volodya—because in him, despite his youth, there was nothing of the boy—no boyish weakness or boyish charm.

There was, in general, no magic about him: there wasn't a hole, there wasn't heat or fever, there wasn't a puzzle, there wasn't a mystery—there was a goal—his own goal for himself.

Such a person shouldn't be either cold or hungry, shouldn't be scared, shouldn't be heartsick. And if all of this happened (and—I think it did), it wasn't my business to hinder him with my tenderness from fighting the cold, hunger, fear, heartsickness: from *growing*.

There was the cold tenderness of a sister, so sure of the strength in her brother, because it was *her* strength, who was blessing him on all journeys. And—on all his journeys.

It was Holy Saturday. Late evening. Killed by people's and friend's indifference, by the emptiness of the house and of my heart (Sonechka had disappeared, Volodya didn't come), I said to Alya:

—Alya! When people like us are so left out by other people, there's no point in thrusting ourselves on God as if we're beggars. He has enough of them without us! We won't go anywhere, to any church, and there'll be no Christ Has Risen[34]—instead, we'll go to bed together—like dogs!

—Yes, yes, of course, my dearest Marina! (*Alya babbled excitedly and with conviction*), to people like us, God himself should come! Because we're shy-beggars, aren't we? Not wanting to blacken his holiday.

Shy or not, dogs or not—we immediately lay down together on our only bed, which used to be a servant's bed, because we lived in the kitchen.

Now I have to explain a little about my house. It was a two-story house and our apartment was on the second floor, but it itself had three levels. Why and how—I can't explain, but it was this way: the bottom floor had a dark hallway, two dark corridors, and a dark dining-room, my room and Alya's large nursery; the top floor had that kitchen and other rooms, and from the kitchen there was an entryway to the attic, or even two attics, first one and then another—one higher than the other. So it turns out there were—four floors.

Everything was huge, spacious, deserted, neglected, multiplied by space and emptiness, and the tone of it all was given by the attic and went down to the second level attic and spread out from there over the whole place to the remotest and, as such, its apparently safe corners.

In the winter of 1919, as I already told you, we—Alya, Irina and I—lived in the kitchen which was—large, wooden, flooded either with sunlight or moonlight, and, when the pipes burst—with water. It had a huge oceanic stove, which we stoked with unfortunate fly-catching paper left by some of our fleeting tenants. (There were tenants—but they always vanished, leaving all their belongings: one left—sticky paper, another—five thousand copies of an unsuccessful portrait of Rosa Luxemburg,[35] others—service jackets and riding breeches . . . And all of it was left—covered with dust till it became transformed and was finally burnt.)

So, it's Holy Saturday, eleven at night. Alya, fully dressed—is fast asleep. I'm also fully dressed, but not asleep. I'm lying, burning up with the bitterness of my first Easter without "Christ Has Risen"—a proof of my dog-like loneliness . . . I, who was trying this whole winter to survive, with the children, the

---

34 In Russian Orthodoxy one says, "Christ Has Risen," accompanied by three kisses, as a greeting on Good Friday and Holy Saturday.

35 Rosa Luxemburg (1871–1919), a Jewish Marxist theorist, philosopher, economist, anti-war activist, and revolutionary socialist of Polish birth, who became a naturalized German citizen.

lines, my trip for the flour where I almost died, my job at Narkomnats,[36] chopping wood, stoking the furnace, and my three plays—I was starting a fourth—and so many poems, and such good ones, and now not even a dog...

Suddenly, there was—a knock. Light, short, sharp. A command of a knock. And as one lump—I get up, and as the same lump—indiscriminately arms and legs—like a vertical stratum, run through the dark kitchen, down the stairs, through the hallways and feel for the bolt—Volodya is on the threshold. I recognize him by his outline, even in the dark and against the dark:

—Volodya, is it you?

—I, Marina Ivanovna, came by to take you to matins.

—Volodya, come in a minute. Let me wake Alya.

Upstairs, I whisper (because it's a big secret and because Christ *hasn't* yet risen): "Alya, Get up! Volodya came. Now we're going to matins."

In the dark I smooth my hair and hers, and quickly carry her down the darker-than-night-itself stairs:

—Volodya, are you still here?

A voice comes from the dining room:

—I think I am, Marina Ivanovna, even though I've lost myself here, it's so dark.

We walk out.

Alya, continuing what she had started, but in the rush, not finished:

—I told you, Marina, that God himself would come to us. So, since God's—a spirit and has no legs, and since we both would have died of fear if we'd seen him...

—What? What's she saying? Volodya asks.

We're already out on the street. I, embarrassed:

—Nothing, she's still partly asleep.

—No, Marina (*comes the weak but clear voice from below*)—I'm not at all asleep. And so, since God himself couldn't come to take us to—church, He sent us Volodya. So we can have even more faith in Him. Right, Volodya?

—That's right, Alechka.

---

36 To get food Tsvetaeva went on a dangerous journey, described in her "Free Passage." Narkomnats (the People's Commissariat of Nationalities), was an organization (1917–1924) that dealt with non-Russian nationalities. Tsvetaeva had to work there for a few months. She writes about it in her essay "My Jobs." Both works are translated in Gambrell, *Earthly Signs*.

The Church of Boris and Gleb,[37] our church. It's white and round like a communion host. In front of it, precisely during the service hours, military exercises took place this whole winter. Inside—there's service, outside—marching: which is also service. But now the soldiers are asleep.

We enter into the warm, crowded, many-candled radiance and unity. Female voices sing, sing thinly—with all their yearning and frailty, it's hard to hear, they're so thin—so thin it's ready to break, almost hair-thin—singing—almost like that professor, who said: "I have only one hair on my head, but it's so thick!" . . . Lord, have mercy! Lord, have mercy! Lord have mercy! . . . I know this priest: not long ago he led the service with the Patriarch, who came for the Patronal Festival[38]—in a black carriage, weak and radiant . . . And Alya ran to him first and simply kissed his hand, and he blessed her . . .

—Marina Ivanovna, shall we go?

We leave with the crowd—only the old women are left in the church.

—Christ is risen, Marina Ivanovna!

—*Indeed* He is risen, Volodya!

Alya returned home in Volodya's arms. Since he's so unused to children, he carries her awkwardly—not up on his back, or in one arm—instead, he's actually carrying her—in his two stretched-out arms, so she's lying and looking up at the sky:

—Alechka, are you comfortable?

—Blissfully so! It's the first time in my life that I'm being carried this way, as if I'm the Queen of Sheba, lying on a stretcher!

(*Volodya, who hadn't expected anything like that, is silent.*)

—Marina, come closer to my ear, I want to say something to you, so Volodya won't hear it, because it's—a big sin! No, no, don't be afraid, it's not what you think! It's all decent, but to God—it isn't!

(*I come closer. She, in a loud whisper:*)

---

37   Boris and Gleb were the first saints canonized in Kiev Rus after the Christianization of the country.

38   Celebrating the foundation of the church.

—Marina, isn't it true that those nuns singing sounded like a fly being sucked out by a spider? God forgive me! God forgive me! God forgive me.
—What's she saying?
(*Alya, rising:*)
—Marina! Don't repeat it! Because if you do Volodya will also be tempted! Because I got this thought from the Devil. Oh, dear God, what did I say again? I used his ugly name!
—(*Volodya*) Alechka, calm down! (*To me:*) Is she always like that?
—From birth.
—Here, Alechka, we're home already, now you'll sleep, and in the morning, when you awake...
In his hand is the dark but clear silhouette of an egg.[39]

Alya is settled and put to bed. Volodya and I stand by the front door:
—Marina Ivanovna, does Alya usually sleep tight?
—Tight indeed. Have no fear, Volodya, she never wakes up!
We go out. Walking. Along the Prechistensky Boulevard toward the Moscow River. We stand on the embankment (everything's like a dream)—looking at the river... And now, when I'm writing, I feel with my top ribs the stone of the balustrade, over which we both, for some unknown reason, leaned too far, so as to discern what: the past? the future? or something existing inside us?

This was the night of banisters, gratings, bridges. We were all the time trying to spy out something—and not spying it out from there—going to the next embankment, next bridge, as if there were a certain place from which—we'd suddenly see everything, clear to the ends of the earth... And maybe—we were saying farewell to all of it—together: the Moscow River, bridges, places, crosses. It seems to me (and maybe tis just a dream of mine[40]) that, on our way to one of our guard-posts, we met Pavlik—who was leaving there, and obviously, also looking for something. (During this Easter Night of 1919, the whole of Moscow was up and walking in approximately the same places—near the Kremlin.)

And maybe we were saying goodbye—to each other? The words of this long, long, many-houred and many-placed night—because we left the house

---

39 A customary gift, symbolizing new life.
40 A slightly altered line from A. Blok's poem, "The unknown woman."

at 1am and returned when it was already the full light of the late spring sunrise day—the words of this night I don't remember. This whole night was—a gesture: his to me. His act—for me.

On this night, in one of those places, above one of the handrails and in a tight shoulder-to-shoulder closeness to me, he made a decision, a decision harder than stone, hardened in him, which cost his life. And it cost me a whole eternity of—friendship, for one hour of which, I, in Aksakov's words,[41] would give the rest of my fading days . . .

How did it all start? (Because at that point, in opposition to those bridges—it started.)

It must have been an accident, lucky and predestined, *in den Sternen geschriebenen*,[42] the coincidence of Sonechka's dropping by—during his visit:

—How come, Volodya, you're here? You—also visit Marina, do you? Marina, I'm jealous! So, you aren't sitting alone when I'm not here?

—And you, Sonechka, do you sit alone when you're not here?

—Me! I'm—a lost case, I sit with everyone. I'm so afraid of death that when no one's around and no one could be around—there are such horrible hours!—I'm ready to climb up to the cat on the roof—as long as I don't have to sit on my own: not to die on my own, Marina!—So, Volodya, what are you doing here?

—The same thing as you, Sophia Evgenevna.

—That means: you love Marina. Because I don't do anything else here or anywhere else in the world. And I'm not intending to do anything else. And it's not in my intention that others should get in my way.

—Sophia Evgenevna, I can leave. Should I leave, Marina Ivanovna?

—No, Volodechka.

—Should *I* leave? (*Sonechka with a dare.*)

—No, Sonechka. (*Pause.*) Well, ladies and gentlemen, should I leave? (*Laughter.*)

—Well, Marina, let's pretend he isn't here. Marina, I'm here from Yura: just imagine, he's getting another gumboil!

---

41 Probably Sergey Timofeyeevich Aksakov (1791–1859), a 19th century Russian literary figure.

42 Written in the stars.

—That means I will have to write him poems again. You know, Sonechka, my first poem to him:

> *Beau ténébreux*,[43] you're sad, you're sick:
> The world's unjustified—you've a toothache! A foulard—
> Dark as night—wraps the tender shell of your cheek...

—A fou-lard? A checkered one? A blue and black one? I gave it to him—a year ago. I remember very well. I had a neckerchief—I awfully love neckerchiefs, and this one I loved especially!—and I came to visit him—and he had a gumboil—and I adore it when someone's sick! Especially when the beautiful ones are sick—then they're kinder . . . (*pause*) . . . when the leopard is quite dying, he's terribly kind, so good-natured!! And he had such a terribly ugly bandage—a knitted one. Nannie's. So I, without having time to think . . . Afterward—I regretted it. It was Papa's foulard, and I've got so few things left—of his . . .

—Sonechka, do you want me to take it from him? Or even steal it?

—Oh, no, Marina, he now loves it terribly: he wears it with every gumboil!

—(*Volodya contemplatively:*) A gumboil is—a non-intellectual disease, Sophia Evgenevna.

—Wha-at? You're such a fool!

—(*Volodya in the same manner:*) Because it comes from a neglected tooth, and neglected teeth in our century . . .

—Go to all the devils! Go the dentists! Not an "intellectual disease"! As if there were such things as—intellectual diseases. A disease is a fate: a human has to die of something, otherwise he'd live forever. Sickness is a fate—and always has been, but your intellectualism started yesterday and will end tomorrow, or is already ended—today. Because look how we all live? Marina with her own hands breaks up the redwood dressers in order to boil a bowl of millet. Is that intellectual?

—But Marina Ivanovna, while breaking up the dressers, remains—an intellectual.

—Which she never was. Isn't it true, Marina, that you've never been an intellectual?

—Never. Not even in my dreams, Sonechka.

---

43 Gloomy good-looker.

—I knew it was so, because all of it: the poems, Marina herself, the blue lamp, and this taxidermized fox are—magical, not intellectual. "An intellectual"—Marina?—that's almost as nonsensical as calling her a "poetess." What a foul thing to say! Oh, how silly you are, Volodya, how silly!

—Sophia Evgenevna, earlier you called me a fool, but "silly" is less bad, so you are . . . diluting the effect.

—And you are only intensifying my fury. Because I'm very angry with you, at your presence. What is there to see at Marina's that you haven't seen? You're an actor, you should be in the studio . . .

(*Pause*)

. . . I don't know who you are for Marina, but—Marina loves me more. Isn't it so, Marina? (*I take her hand and kiss it.*) Well, see, I told you—more. Because Marina has never kissed your hand, has she? And if you say that she has . . .

—(*Volodya*) Sophia Evgenevna!—

— . . . then she did it out of pity, because you're—a man, a wordless creature, an inanimate object, the only inanimate object in the whole of grammar! You see, I know, why we kiss a man's hands! Marina expressed it once and forever, "Ta-ta-ta-ta . . . O my infirmity and my deity—forgive my tears!" Only, isn't it right, Marina—first deity and then—infirmity?! (*Almost crying.*) And Marina, if I ask her, will kick you out. Right, Marina?

—(*I, kissing her other hand:*) No, Sonechka.

—And if she won't kick you out, it's only because she's polite, well-brought up, brought up abroad, but inside—she kicked you out as soon as I walked in. So, clear out, please. This is—my place.

—Sonechka, you're a real little devil today!

—And did you think that—I was always as silky, velvety, chocolaty, creamy with everyone, as I am with you? Oho! You see, as Vakhtang Levanovich told you, I am—a devil? Devil, I am. In any case—I'm as mad as a devil. Volodya, do you know how to start a gramophone?

—I do, Sophia Evgenevna.

—Please, put on the first thing there is—so I don't have to hear myself.

The first thing was "Ave Maria"—Gounod.[44] And here I, with my own eyes, saw a miracle, in the effect of the music—on the devil. Because with its first sounds the wild cat with unsheathed claws and a bared-teeth little snout,

---

44 Charles-François Gounod (1818–1893), a French composer.

which Sonechka was from the moment of Volodya's arrival—disappeared, dissolving at first into the question in her own huge eyes, which couldn't discern Volodya or me any longer, and then into her response—bursting into tears.

—Dear God, what is it? I know that I know it, it's—some sort of heaven!

—It's "Ave Maria," Sonechka!

—Could this really be on the gramophone? I thought that on the gramophone there was only—"an apache dance"[45] or maybe—a tango.

—This is *my* gramophone, Sonechka, it can play anything. Volodechka, turn the record over.

On the other side was—a violin version of Glinka's, "Don't Tempt Me Needlessly,"[46] no words, but conveying the clear meaning of Baratynsky's undying lines—clearer and fuller than if the words had been uttered.[47]

—Marina, I know this one too! Papa played it—when he was still well... And I fell asleep to it throughout my whole early childhood! "Don't Tempt Me Needlessly"... how marvelous that "needlessly" is, because nobody says it in real life, only *there* they say it, where there is already no need of anything—in heaven, Marina! And I myself am now in heaven, Marina. We are all in heaven! And this taxidermized fox is in heaven, and this wolf-like carpet is in heaven, and the lamppost and the gramophone, all—in heaven...

—And in heaven (*Volodya's quiet voice responds*), Sophia Evgenevna, there's no jealousy and everyone forgives each other, because they see there was nothing to forgive, because it wasn't—anyone's fault... And there are no reserved seats: everyone has his own. And now, Marina Ivanovna, I'll go.

(*Sonechka, in tears:*)

—No, no, Volodya, not for anything in the world. How can anyone leave—after such music?—all alone—after such music, away from Marina—after such music... (*pause, barely audibly*)—and from me... I'll never forgive myself, my behavior today! Because, you see, I thought you were simply—an empty good-looker—and that you, like everyone, go to Marina so she'll write poems to you and you can boast afterward!

—Marina Ivanovna never wrote a line to me. Isn't it so, Marina Ivanovna?

---

45 A dramatic dance associated with the Parisian street culture of the early twentieth century.

46 Mikhail Ivanovich Glinka (1804–1857), the first Russian composer to gain wide recognition in his own country.

47 Yevgeny Abramovich Baratynsky (1800–1844), lauded by Pushkin as the finest Russian elegiac poet.

—That's the truth, Volodechka.

—Marina, doesn't it mean that you *don't* love him?

—(*I half-jokingly*:) I love him so much that I can't even say how much. Even in poems—I can't.

—More or less than Yura?

—(*Volodya:*) Sophia Evgenevna!

—(*She:*) Forget that you are in the room right now. I just need to know this instant.

—(*I reply:*) Yury Alexandrovich wasn't a friend for even an hour; Volodya is my friend for life. I called him Volodya from the first minute and I never once called Yury Alexandrovich—Yura, except when talking about him and in his absence.

—(*Sonechka, intently and even painedly*:) More or less, though? More or less?

—Volodya immeasurably more. Full stop.

—And now, Marina Ivanovna, I'll definitely leave.

———

And—so it went on. If before that they'd never met one another at my place, now they started to do it—all the time, maybe it was because Volodya used to come rarely, but now he started to come every other evening. At last, though, he came every evening—because the affair was obviously moving to a not-yet-named, but known, end.

The departures started—with Irina:

—Let me, mistress, take Irina with me to the village—look at her, she's puny. And no wonder—who can put on weight from Soviet milk? (This is what the children in Moscow of 1919 called water.) There we have—country milk. It was white under the Tsar and, without him, it's still white, and the potatoes are fresh, not frozen, and the bread is without lime. And when Irina returns to you—she'll be as fat as tha-at.

In the kitchen: the sun shines through two windows. As skinny as a pole stands our Vladimir nanny, Nadya, with Irina dressed up in her arms. In front of them is—Sonechka, who ran by to say farewell:

—Well, Irina, please, grow into a big, beautiful, and happy girl!

—(*Irina, with a sly smile:*) Halli-dah! Halli-dah!

—May your little cheeks be rosy pink, your little eyes never cry, your little hands hold and not let go, your little feet run . . . and you never fall . . .

Irina, who had never seen tears, in any case tears like that, catches them unceremoniously from Sonechka's eyes:

—We-et... we-etsies, eyes we-et...

—Yes, they're wet because they are—tears... tears. But don't repeat it, you don't need to know that word...

—Miss Sophia Evgenevna, it's time for us to go to the train station, Irina and I are—on foot, and won't make it inside an hour.

—Okay, Nanny, okay. What else can I say to her, so she understands? Yes, Nanny, please, make sure that she prays to God every morning and evening—simply like this: Dear God, please show mercy to Papa, Mama, Alya, Nanny...

—(*Irina:*)... Halli-dah! Halli-dah!

—And for Hallidah too, because she never calls me Sonya and I don't want her to forget me. I've never loved a child the way I love you.—And for Hallidah (God will know!).—Nanny, you won't forget?

—What are you saying, Sophia Evgenevna, besides Irina herself will remind me and will even buzz my ears off with Hallidah...

—(*Irina, understanding something, responded with incredible spirit:*) Halli-dah, Halli-dah, Halli-dah, Halli-dah, Halli-dah... (*and then teasingly:*) Dalligah, Dalligah, Dalligah...

—God be with you, Irina! That's the way you'll talk to Baba-Yaga![48]—And you're saying—she'll forget you! Now she won't stop the whole way! Well, say goodbye, Sophia Evgenevna, or we'll really be late!

—Farewell, my dear little girl! Little hand... another one... your little leg... another one... little eye... another one... your forehead—and that's it, because no kiss on the lips is allowed. And you, Nanny, also don't let her be kissed on the lips, say—mistress won't allow it—and that's that. Well, goodbye my girl! (*Crosses her three times.*) I'll be praying for you too. Get well, come back healthy, beautiful, red-cheeked. Nanny, take care of her!

I'll tell you right away that Irina will never again see her Hallidah, or Hallidah her Irina. This was their last meeting. June 7, 1919.

But about five months later Irina, whom Sonechka left at the age of two years and three months, still remembered her Hallidah, as can be seen from Alya's journal entry—of November 1919:

---

48 A fairytale witch.

"We have one friend, who isn't in Moscow now. Her name is Sophia Evgenevna Holliday. We call her Sonechka and when she isn't there, Sonechka Holliday. Irina took an instant liking to her. Sonechka left even earlier and Irina still remembers her and even now she says and sings: Hallidah! Hallidah!"

—Volodechka, you've never been in Marina's kitchen, have you?

—No, Sophia Evgenevna. Well, maybe once, during Easter.

—God, I feel so sorry for you! You've never seen Irina?

—No, Sophia Evgenevna, I haven't. Well, maybe once, that same time—but she was asleep.

—Dear God, how can one be friends with a woman and not know how many teeth her child has? You probably *don't* know how many teeth Irina has, do you?

—No, I don't, Sophia Evgenevna.

—Then, this is all just mental, you're friends only with Marina's head.—God, who was it, with only *one* head?

—You and me, Sophia Evgenevna.

—Fool! I'm saying with *only* a head, with nothing else ... Ah, it's in *Ruslan and Ludmila!*[49] How cold I'd be from such a friendship! It's such an ice-house ... Oh, how much happier I am, Volodya! I also have a downstairs Marina, a crystal one, and a lamppost one that's—under the blue light as if underwater, because, you see, this is—the bottom of the sea, and all its guests are—water monsters! And a top floor Marina, above the stove, above the millet, with an axe, with the hem of her brown dress sawed through, which I—here—kiss!—Marina who is respected and adored! And you see, both of these are Marina, all of them are—Marina, because I don't see you, Marina—only in a castle, only in a tower ...

—(*I:*) In my free time I'd be tending rams ...

—(*Volodya*) And listening—to voices.

By the way Sonechka started with Volodya I came remotely to understand why men don't like her. Any misunderstanding, any contradiction, even a very modest attempt to state their own opinion, provoked her unchangeable

---

49 A poem Pushkin published in 1820, which was made into an opera by Glinka.

response: fool! As if that word "fool" was loaded and waiting for a signal, which could be—anything. With her, one had to have patience and not notice—you had to have Volodya's patience and his ability not to notice.

I always saw her off to the right, the Povarskaya Street direction. Sonechka leaving was for me a sun-rise on Povarskaya, which was a white street without shops, which looked like a river—it was as if there was no *left* turn from my house.

Only once was it different. It was nighttime and I realized that I hadn't yet shown my fountain to Sonechka.

In this completely empty, toy-like, moonlit square, which is Dog Square in the daytime and now seemed like—a Square in Seville, where the only living thing was a circle of saplings, like a double thin silver rivulet, one for the ear and one for the eye—surrounding one in silver...

—A fountain, Marina?

—*Marina's* fountain, Sonechka! Because in this house Pushkin read his *Godunov* to Naschokin.[50]

—I don't like *Godunov*. I like *Don Giovanni*.[51] Oh, how everything here is so round, round, round!

And—as if she was carried by a wind—taken by a wave—somehow without her legs' participation—she was already in the middle of the square.

And there, with one of her arms on the shoulder of an invisible and very tall dancer, and with the other trustfully placed in his hand, she slightly leaned her torso on *his* invisible left hand, slightly raised on her tiptoes to compensate for the absence of heels, surrounded by a white dress and fanning me with it...

She was dancing around the fountain, as if around an urn—she was dancing around the urn as if dancing around death...

Das Mädchen und der Tod.[52]

---

50   *Boris Godunov*, one of Pushkin's *Little Tragedies*. Pavel Voinovich Naschokin (1801–1854), a Russian philanthropist, art collector, and a close friend of Pushkin's during the last years of his life.

51   Another of Pushkin's *Little Tragedies*.

52   A song, later a quartet, by Franz Schubert (1797–1828), based on a poem by the German poet Matthias Claudius (1740–1815).

—Marina, everything I have is diminutive, everybody—diminutive: all my girlfriends, my things, cats, even men, like all these diminutive Katen'kas, kittens, nannykins, Yurochkas, Pavliks, and now—Volodechka . . . It's as if I don't dare pronounce anything big. Only you are my—*Marina*, so huge, so long . . . Oh, Marina! You are my—superlative!

Sonechka often thought out loud, and I always recognized this by her absent, impossibly wide-open, sleepy eyes, the eyes of our first meeting ("Do such snowstorms and such loves really happen . . .")

In moments like this she froze and her voice became monotone, chanting, sleepy like her eyes, a voice mothers use to lull their children to sleep and children use—themselves. (And sometimes mothers use—to lull themselves to sleep.) And if she replied—to my or Volodya's comments—she did it somehow without being aware of herself, as if in a dream, without any intonation, like a real somnambulist. No, she wasn't *thinking* aloud, but—dreaming aloud.

—And there's one sort of man I've never loved yet—a monk. I've never had the chance.

—Ugh, Sonechka!

—No, Marina, don't think that—I'm not talking about a Russian Orthodox bearded one, but about one with a shaved head: a Catholic one. Maybe a very young one, or maybe one already very old—it doesn't matter. In a huge, cellar-cold monastery, this monk lives alone—there was a plague, you see, and everyone died. They died out and he was left alone to live—and do God's work. One, out of the whole Order. The last one. And this whole Order is now—him.

—Sophia Evgenevna (*in a sober voice, Volodya's voice*) please, let me tell you that this Monastery isn't the whole Order. The Order can't die out because the monastery did. Only the monastery can die out, but not the Order.

—The last one from the whole Order, because all the monasteries died out . . . Two thousand three hundred and thirty-three monasteries died out because it's the Middle Ages and there's a plague . . . And I—a peasant girl, in a white kerchief, striped skirt, and a bodice like this—with crossed ribbons—I'm the only one who survived out of the whole village—because the monks plagued all around (oh, Marina, I'm madly afraid of them! I'm talking about the Catholic ones: birds, like devils of some sort!)—and so I bring milk to him at the monastery—milk from the last she-goat which didn't yet die—and simply put it by the entrance to his cell...

—And your monk—drinks milk? (*Volodya asks with curiosity*) Because they're sometimes—fasting...

—... And one day when I come to him—yesterday's milk wasn't even touched. With a beating heart, I walked into the cell—the monk lies there—and I see him for the first time: he's very young—or slightly old, but *shaved*—and I'm madly in love with him—and I understand that he has—the plague.

(*Suddenly leaping up, jumping and waking up:*)

—No! This way the whole story is already over, and he didn't have time to love me, because when there's plague—there's no time for love. No, it's not that way. *First* love, then—plague! Marina, how do I do it so it turns out—*that way*?

—See the monk a day before the plague. On his last normal day. A day is a lot, Sonechka!

—But how do I know the plague will come tomorrow? And if I don't know, I won't dare tell him, because I'm only telling him because he's about to die, and he listens to me only because he's deathly weak!

—(*Volodya, contemplatively:*) The plague starts with a stuffed nose. People sneeze.

—Sneezing, that's—the doctor's plague, but mine is—Pushkin-like,[53] nobody sneezed there, but everyone drank and kissed. Isn't it so, Marina?

—Go to confess to him: you must tell everything there and he has to listen. This is not a sin, but a Christian duty.

—Oh, Marina! You're... you're—such a genius! So, I come to him in the chapel—he's praying—the only one from the whole Order. I kneel...

—(*Volodya*: And he's kneeling and you're kneeling? It doesn't flow. You'll bump foreheads.)

—And he—gets up and I... don't: "Brother, I'm a great sinner!" And he asks me: "Why?" And I say, "Because I love you." And he says, "God commanded us to love everyone." And I reply, "No, no, not that way, like everyone, but more than everyone, more than anyone, even more than God!" And he: "Oh! My dear sister, I can't hear any of this. There is a huge wind in my ears, because I've contracted the plague!"—and suddenly he reels—leans—and I support him and feel how his heart is beating through his cassock, beating

---

53 One of Pushkin's *Little Tragedies* is *The Feast During the Plague*.

madly! beating madly!—and so I lead him, take him out of the chapel, and not to his cell but to a green meadow where at this moment the first little tree is blooming—we sit under this blooming little tree—I put his head in my lap . . . and sing—"Ave Maria" to him quietly, Marina! And I sound weaker and weaker, because I too have contracted—the plague—but God is merciful and we *don't* suffer, and I've such a marvelous voice—God, what a marvelous voice I have!—and now not just one tree is blooming, but all of them, because they're in a hurry, because they know we've got—the plague!—there's a whole blooming procession, as if we're getting married!—and we're already not sitting, but walking hand-in-hand, and not on the ground, but a bit above it, above the forget-me-nots, and the further we go—the higher we get—now we are a half a yard above the ground, then a whole yard, Marina, then two yards above it! and now we are walking above the little trees . . . above the clouds. (*Very quietly and questioningly*:) Can we walk above the stars?

(*Wiping her eyes and from her whole soul*:)
—There, Marina, I've now loved a monk!

———————

— . . . But I have to live with others—with different people! Because my monk understood everything immediately—and forgave—and corrected it, without my saying anything. But no matter how much I say, Marina, or try to explain it all, jumping out of my skin, my eyes, lips—nobody understands, not even Evgeny Bagartionovich—with his notorious "imagination"!

However, he has his reasons. In the beginning of our acquaintance, I disgraced myself terribly. When we started talking about images at our Studio.

—Sacred images,[54] Sonechka?

—No, about images. Being—the image of someone. Who is the image—and who isn't, etc. And I say: "Evgeny Bagartionovich, in my opinion, is the image of Pechorin."[55] Everyone replies: "That's—silly! Pechorin was—a hundred years ago, and Evgeny Bagartionovich is—modernity itself, the theater of the future, etc." So I say: "Then I didn't understand. I wasn't talking about ideas, but about a face—'man was created in the image and likeness.'[56] And this

---

54   The word *óbraz* means both an image and a sacred image.
55   The main character in Lermontov's *A Hero of Our Time* (1840, revised 1841).
56   Genesis 1:27.

is why I think that Evgeny Bagartionovich looks awfully like Pechorin, with his nose, his chin, and his hemorrhoidal complexion."

—(*I*) Wha-at?

—(*Sonechka, meekly:*) That's what I said, Marina, exactly those words. Immediately, there was a great shout. They jumped on me, even Evgeny Bagartionovich: "Sophia Evgenevna, everything has a limit, even your tongue." But I—insist: "What's so bad about it? I constantly read it in Chekhov and in Potapenko.[57] There's no point in being insulted by it if such great writers . . ."—"And what do you think hemorrhoidal means?"—"Well, yellow, jaundiced, bitter, disappointed—in other words—hemorrhoidal."—"No, Sophia Evgenevna, it's *not* yellow, not jaundiced, not bitter, not proud, it's—an illness."—"Yes, yes, and an unhealthy one, it's from a liver disease. That's probably why I said—Pechorin."—"No, Sophia Evgenevna, it isn't a liver disease, but hemorrhoids. Haven't you ever read about it in the newspapers?"—"I did and what's more . . ."—"No, please—no more, because in the newspapers—there are so many diseases, one is more unmentionable than another. And *my* advice to you: before you say anything . . ."—"But I so felt this word! It seemed to me so pensive, magic, all yellow—almost brown—like you!"

Afterward it was explained to me. Oh, Marina, what a shame it was! And the most important thing, I've used this word so often in my life, but I couldn't remember with whom . . .

But I think that Evgeny Bagartionovich still didn't completely believe that—I didn't know. Well, he probably believed me then, but afterward somehow didn't trust me on the whole. When I *very* much want to say something, he—it's very visible when it happens!—looks at my mouth so especially—disapprovingly and peremptorily—like a snake at a bird. As if—by his glance he could close it—immediately! And if he could—he'd do it with his hand!

A little more about words:

—Everyone here now says: revolution . . . revolution . . . but I don't know . . . Only, they're very weird—these words: *consumer-goods coupon* is like *ocean-going ship*. I, right away, see wa-ter, nothing but wa-ter . . . Well, and there's actually nothing you get with this coupon except water . . . Or—another example: *closed-to-the-public distribution center*? That's a locked-in, deaf-as-

---

57   Ignaty Nikolayevich Potapenko (1856–1929), a Russian writer and playwright.

a-post old man, I say to him: "Dedushka!" And he replies: "Eh?"—"Distribute please!" And he replies: "E-eh!" And it's this way for hours ... And another word, *jagra*. It sounds like plague, famine, scurvy, but it's nothing but—carrot tea.[58]

— ... Marina! Why do I love bad poems so much, while so much loving—yours, Pavlik's, Pushkin's, and Lermontov's ... "In high noon's heat"?—Marina, how much it *burns*! I always imagine myself being him and her, and I lie, Marina, in Dagestan valley,[59] and my wound is—smoking, and at the same time, Marina, I'm in the maidens' circle alone in pensive thought ...

> My youthful soul was caught it seemed,
> Lord God knows how, in some sad dream: ...[60]

---

58   Used during the Revolution in place of real tea.
59   Located in the North Caucasus region.
60   Sonechka is talking about Lermontov's famous poem, "The Dream" (1843):

> In high noon's heat in a Caucasian valley
> I lay quite still, a bullet in my breast;
> The smoke was rising from my deep wound,
> As drop by drop out flowed my blood.
>
> I lay alone on the valley's sand;
> The mountain ledges closed in around,
> Sun burned their yellow peaks
> It burned me, too, but deep as death I slept.
>
> I dreamt I saw the shining lights
> Of evening feasting in my homeland.
> Young maids with flowers in their hair
> Spoke gaily of me amongst themselves.
>
> But one maid sat apart in thought
> And did not enter gaily in
> Her youthful soul was caught it seemed,
> Lord God knows how, in some sad dream:
>
> She dreamt about a Caucasus' valley;
> She knew the corpse upon the ground;
> His breast was blackened by a smoking wound,
> His cooling blood flowed in a stream.

All the poems that were ever written in the world are—about me, Marina, for me, Marina, to me, Marina! That's why I don't ever regret that I don't write them... Marina, you're—a poet, tell me, is it really important—who does it? Is there such a—*who*? (Now, now, now, I'm at my wits end! But you'll understand!) Marina, it isn't really you—who wrote it all? I know your hand did. And when I look at it, I always restrain myself with a huge effort from kissing it—in front of people, not because those idiots would see slavishness in it, a female student's exaltation and hysterics, but because your hands, Marina, must be kissed—in front of *everyone* who is, was, and will be, and not just in front of three or four friends. And if I, after this Dickens-like night, in front of Pavlik, accidentally kissed them, it was—weakness, Marina, I just couldn't keep myself from doing it—couldn't hold in my gratitude. But Pavlik really doesn't count, Marina—he's a poet himself and slightly like a dog, I want to say, he isn't a complete person—from *both sides*... (And you, Volodya, also don't count: see, I kiss them in front of you, but you don't count—because I've already decided so: when the three of us are together it's still as if there's only Marina and I...) And once, in front of everyone at the S-v's,[61] it was worse. But you so marvelously responded to that fox-terrier of a person—without even turning a hair... I kissed your hand, your *hands*—for the whole of you, not just for your poems, but also for the wardrobes you chop up with your hands—for that even more! I'm always insulted when they say that you are a "great poet," and more so when they say a "genius." It's Pavlik who's—a "genius," because there's nothing else in his soul, whereas you, you've got everything, the whole of you. And compared to you, Marina, with what you—wholly are, your poems are—just a small thing, a pitiful little drop—you aren't insulted, are you? Sometimes I want to laugh when they call you a poet. Even though there's nothing higher than this word. And maybe nothing higher—than this craft. But some things are—higher. And all of them are—you. If you didn't write any poems, not even a tiny line, if you were deaf and mute, mute—like the Little Mermaid and me, you'd still be—the same, only with a sewn-up mouth. And I'd be loving you—no, not more, because there is—no more, but absolutely the same as now—on my knees.

(*With her head already on my knees*:)

—Marina! Do you know what was my biggest heroic deed? Even bigger than with that red-nosed one (the organ-grinder), because *not* to do is much

---

61   An unknown reference.

more difficult than *to do*: after *Snowstorm*, I still didn't kiss your hand! Not out of fear of being slavish, no, nor of other people's eyes, but out of—fear—of you, Marina, fear of losing you at once, or getting you at once (what a foul word "getting" is, and "acquiring," "gaining," "conquering"—all foul!), or the other way around—fear of you, Marina, well, fear of the Lord, whatever it's called, no, not fear of the Lord, no, even that isn't it: fear to turn the key, to swallow poison—and for something to start that it's impossible to stop … A fear of *that*, Marina! Of "open, Sesame!" Marina, and forgetting the word for getting back! And never being able to get out of this mountain … Being buried alive in this mountain … which in addition will collapse on you …

Simply—fear of your fear, Marina. How could I know? For my whole life, Marina, I was the only one like this: word, deed, and thought were—all the same and at once, simultaneous, as if I'd never had word, deed, thought, but only … some sort of electrical discharge!

Now, about *Snowstorm*. When I first heard with my own ears:

> —Count, is it a dream—or a sin?
> —Poor scared baby-bird!
> —I was the *first* one, before *everyone else*
>   To hear your horse bells![62]

This "first" and "before everyone else," uttered with the same emphasis as I'd have uttered them, as if taken out of my mouth—Marina! Everything inside of me—fluttered, fluttered as if alive, you'd laugh, but my whole stomach and my gullet, all of those mysterious inner organs, which nobody has ever seen—it was as if all my insides—from my throat to my knees—were pearls, and had suddenly—all of them—come alive.

And so why is it, Marina, that, loving your poems so much, I ma-dly, ma-dly, so hopelessly, so disgracefully, so shamefully love—bad ones. Oh, completely bad ones! Not Nadson[63] (I worship him!) and not Apukhtin[64] (for his "Dark eyes"!), but the ones nobody ever wrote down and everyone knows. Poems from *The Reader-Reciter*,[65] Marina, now do you understand?

---

62 The first line and the final two are spoken by the Lady in the cloak, the second by the Gentleman in the cloak.
63 Semyon Yakovlevich Nadson (1862–1887), a Russian Empire poet.
64 Aleksey Nikolayevich Apukhtin (1840–1893), a Russian poet, writer, and critic.
65 A collection of poems published monthly for home entertainment.

> He picked her up from the very dirt.
> To please her—he became a thief.
> Now drowning in prosperity,
> She laughed at him and called him mad.
>
> He begged her from the prison walls:
> Without you my soul is stole!
> In a troika she went driving by
> And laughed at him and called him mad.

And in the end—he was taken to the hospital, and—

> On his deathbed she danced,
> Drank wine and gaily laughed.

(Oh, I'd kill her!) And I think when he died and was taken to the graveyard, she—

> Behind his coffin walked—laughing!

But maybe I've made up the last part, so I could hate her even more. Because I've never seen anything like it: to walk in a funeral procession—and laugh, have you?

But perhaps you think that one isn't bad? Then listen. Oh, God, I forgot! forgot! forgot! forgot how it starts, I only remember the end!

> The Count was devilishly good-looking!
> ...
> And I in darkness sharpened my knife—
> The Count was devilishly good-looking!

Wait, wait, wait!

> The red curtain rose:
> And in his arms her sister lay!

Here she kills them both, and now, in the last verse, her sister lies down with bared teeth, awful face, and—the Count is such a devilish good-looker!

And do you know—"The pale-yellow rose"? He meets her in the park or maybe at the church, she's sixteen and in a white dress...

> And a pale-yellow rose
> Was trembling on your breast.

Then, she, of course, becomes dissipated, and he sees her at a restaurant with some officer, and suddenly she sees him too!

> The tears trembled in your eyes
> You screamed, 'Give me wine! And fast!'
> And a pale-yellow rose
> Was trembling on your breast.
>
> The days had passed one by one,
> I sought for comfort in oblivion,
> And once again in front of me
> Your earlier dear glance I see.
>
> The prose of family had seized you,
> You walk with a throng of children blest,
> And a pale-yellow rose
> Was trembling on your breast.

And then she dies, Marina, and lies in her coffin, and he comes to it and sees that:

> In your eyes the tears had frozen

—and then, I don't know what else was on her—

> And a pale-yellow rose
> Was trembling on your breast.

Trembling, understand, on the non-breathing breast! But—I love it madly, and the throng of children, his suspicious comfort, the pale-yellow rose, and the grave.

But that isn't all, Marina. That one is still—somehow—tolerable, because somehow sad. But there is such nonsense that I love *madly*. Do you know *this one*?

> She was born,
> Christened,
> Married,
> Received a blessing.
>
> She gave birth,
> She christened,
> She married
> She gave a blessing—
> died.

This is the whole of—a woman's life!
Do you know *this one*?

> My quill was scribbling, writing
> I do not know to whom . . .'

I:

> But then my heart was telling
> That it was to my dear groom.

Sonechka:

> —I give you now this puppy
> And ask you it to love
> And it will teach you how
> Your dear friend to love.

—Love—to love—are these real poems, Marina? Even I can do it. But I see in it—this quill—definitely a goose one, all gnawed to shreds, and a little puppy, Marina, with curly ears, silver-chocolate colored, and eyes ready to cry: I myself sometimes have such eyes.

And now, Marina, at last, my most favorite one. I'm saying it seeeriously. (*With a dare in her voice:*) Mo-re fa-vo-rite than yours.

> A blue ball is spinning and turning around
> Spinning and turning above head and ground.
> Spinning and turning, and ready to drop,
> The chevalier wants this damsel kidnapped.

No, Marina! I can't! I'll sing it—to you!

(*She jumps up, lifts her head and sings the same thing. Then, coming close to me and standing above me:*)

—Now tell me, Marina, do you—understand that? Can you love me, like that? Because this is my most favorite poem. Because it is (*closed eyes*) simply—bliss. (*Reciting as if she's asleep:*)—A ball in the blue spinning, an air balloon of Montgolfier,[66] in a net of blue silk, and the ball is—blue, and the sky is—blue, and the one who looks at it is scared out of his mind that the ball will

---

66 Joseph-Michel Montgolfier (1740–1810) and Jacques-Étienne Montgolfier (1745–1799), the inventors of the first hot air balloon.

fly away forever! And the ball, because of his stare, starts spinning even more, ready to fall any minute, and all the Montgolfiers will perish! Meanwhile, using a good moment when someone is busy with the ball...

The chev-al-ier wants this dam-sel kid-napped.

What could be added to this?

—What about this, Sonechka?

> The curtain shivered
> The room echoes the steps
> Of a blue chevalier
> And his servant...[67]

Everything is there for you too, except the damsel—and the ball. But the ball, Sonechka, is—the *earth*, and he's going—away from his damsel. She's left behind, finished. He had *already* kidnapped her and then saw that—there was no need.

—(*Sonechka, jealously:*) Why?

—(*I:*) Because he was a poet, who doesn't need to kidnap a thing in order to have it. He doesn't need—to have.

—But if *I* was that damsel—would he leave me too?

—No. Sonechka.

—Oh, Marina! How much I love pain! Even—a simple headache! Because I don't at all know toothache. I've never had it. And sometimes I'm ready to cry because my teeth never hurt. People say it's a ma-arvelous pain: a te-di-ous one!

—Sonechka, you're simply mad! Knock on wood, you little she-devil! Do you know Malibran?[68]

—No.

—She was a singer.

—She died?

---

67 A poem by Blok.
68 See part I, note 80.

—She died young, about a hundred years ago. And so Musset wrote poems to her, "Stanzas to Malibran"—listen (*I changed a few words to make it "to Sonechka"*):

> Didn't you know, imprudent comedienne,
> That those frenzied cries which came from the heart
> Made your thinning cheeks grow paler?
> Didn't you know that on your ardent temple,
> Your hand from day to day became more burning,
> And that to love suffering is to tempt God?[69]

There are strange coincidences. This summer of 1937 at the ocean, in the midst of writing *Sonechka*, I picked up in one of the local shops, named *Souvenirs*, which at the same time is a library, an annual called *Lectures* (year 1867), and the first thing I saw was, Ernest Legouvé, "Sixty Years of Recollections: Malibran"[70] (about whom I didn't know much before, with the exception of Musset's poem):

"Despite the fact that she was the very image of life, and that the dominant feature of her character was charm, the idea of death never left her. She always said that she would die young. Sometimes, as if she had suddenly felt an icy breath, as if the shadow of the other world had been projected onto her soul, she fell into a frightful fit of melancholy, and her heart drowned in a deluge of tears. I have before my eyes the words written by her hand: 'Come and see me at once! I suffocate with sobs! All the funeral presences are by my bedside and death at their head...'"[71]

---

69   ... *Ne savais-tu donc pas, comédienne imprudente,*
          Que ces cris insensés qui te sortaient du coeur
          De ta joue amaigrie augmentaient la chaleur?
          Ne savais-tu donc pas que sur ta tempe ardente,
          Ta main de jour en jour se posait plus brûlante,
          Et que c'est tenter Dieu que d'aimer la douleur?

       Alfred Louis Charles de Musset-Pathay (1810–1857), a French dramatist, poet, and novelist. Tsvetaeva changes *chaleur* ("hotter") to *pâleur* ("paler").

70   Gabriel Jean Baptiste Ernest Wilfrid Legouvé (1807–1903), a French dramatist.

71   *Quoiqu'elle fût l'image même de la vie et que l'enchantement pût passer pour un des traits dominants de son caractère, l'idée de la mort lui etait toujours présente. Elle disait toujours qu'elle mourrait jeune. Parfois comme si elle eût senti tout à coup je ne sais quel souffle glacé, comme si l'ombre de l'autre monde se fût projetée dans son âme, elle tombait dans d'affreux accès de mélancolie et son coeur se noyait dans un déluge de larmes. J'ai là sous les yeux ces mots écrits*

What is that, if not one of Sonechka's alive "little notes"?

There were meetings—every evening, without being planned. The two came separately and at different times, from different theaters, from different lives. And Sonechka always wanted—to stay longer, to leave last. But since it meant her—not going home with Volodya, I insisted every time that they should leave—together:
—Go, Sonechka, otherwise I'll inevitably have to see you off, and I'll get stuck at your place, and Alya will be hungry, and so on . . . Go, my joy, because the day will be—over soon!
It was good and safe to let them go—into the sunrise.
Sometimes I walked with them into the sunrise to the corner of Borisoglebsky Lane and Povarskaya Street.
"Love each other well, who have both loved me, and sometimes say my name in a kiss."[72]

—Marina! It turns out that Volodya is—in love! As soon as they saw that I was—*like that* with him—because I talk about him all the time: so as to say his name—they told me at once that recently he hadn't—for the whole evening—taken his eyes off the dancer—who danced on the table at Café Electrician, and didn't even finish his drink.
When I found this out, I immediately said to him: "Volodya, aren't you ashamed of yourself, you visit Marina and feast your eyes on that dancer! In each sleeve of Marina's fustian dress are—a hundred houries and fairies! You're simply—a fool!" I immediately told him that I'd tell you for sure, and he got very scared, Marina, and darkened, and became angry, so angry! And do you know what he said to me? He said: "I always thought that you are *like that* only with Marina Ivanovna and *she* with you. And now I know it." And he

---

de sa main:—*Venez me voir tout de suite! J'étouffe de sanglots! Toutes les idées funèbres sont à mon chevet et la mort—à leur tête.*

72 "*Aimez-vous bien, vous qui m'avez aimée tous deux, et dites-vous parfois mon nom dans un baiser . . .*"

walked away. Now you'll see in what condition he'll come to see you, with his tail between his legs!

He came, not with his tail between his legs, but worried and right away said:

—Marina Ivanovna, you should understand this tale of Sophia Evgenevna's as you've always understood me.

—Volodya! Did I explain Z-sky to you? There is a fairytale—a Norwegian one, I think—called "Whatever the Old Man Does is Good." And the old man is constantly doing foolish things: exchanging a bar of gold for a horse, a horse for a goat, and so on, and finally a cat for a spool, a spool for a needle, and then he loses the needle by his house, while climbing over the wattle fence—because he didn't think to walk through the gate. So, let us be that old man to each other, that is: as long as *he's*—happy, and as long as he returns in *one piece*! Besides, I myself could easily stare at a dancer for three minutes—as long as she doesn't speak.

Volodya! How disgusting it would be if this fairytale went—contrariwise, that is—a needle for a spool, a spool for a sheep and finally, a horse for a bar of gold? Oh, what a rotten old man he would be!

—A lousy old man, Marina Ivanovna! Moscow is full of such "old men" now. From them I'm . . . No, Marina Ivanovna, I wasn't "feasting my eyes" on her. I was—thinking on her. Here the whole world has crashed, there's nothing left from the old one, but this—is forever: a table—and on it a dancing emptiness, dancing—against all this, an emptiness against—all this: against all this *lesson*.

—Such people are said to be—beloved . . .

—If I ever got married—it would be only to a nurse of mercy. So *human* blood—will flow in my children.

—Marina, if only you knew how Volodya kisses—so hard! So hard (*with a sly grin*)—as if I'm a wall! My face was burning all day today.

I'll tell you that to my joy he'd never attempted to explain his relationship with Sonechka. He knew that I knew that it was in this case—his final step *toward me*, that it was—a rapprochement, not a separation, and that in kissing her, he kissed me—kissed all three of us—himself, her, and me—

we three together in the whole Spring of 1919—in her person, on her little face—kissed.

Any attempt to explain it in *words*—would be an insult and the end.

And—Sonechka? She babbled and chirped, declined, conjugated, added, multiplied, and seeded Volodya far and wide in her speech, she was simply made happy by him being around, innocently—as on the first day of creation.

We sat—in the following way: Volodya on the left, myself on the right, in the middle—Sonechka, the two of us—with Sonechka in the middle, we adults—with a child in the middle, we loving ones—with love in the middle. We were embracing, of course: we, with our hands on each other's shoulders, she in us, in our faraway embrace, dividing and bringing us closer, while giving each of us a hand and, to each of us, all of herself, all her love, with her little body erasing the mile that used to separate mine and Volodya's.

Sonechka sat in us, as if in a chair—with a live back, in a *wicker* chair, made of our interlaced arms. Sonechka laid in us, as in a cradle, like Moses in a wicker basket on the waters of the Nile.

And a gramophone from its dark corner, stretching to us its burgundy wooden mouth, sang and played for us everything it knew—everything we "knew": our youth, our love, our heartsickness, our separation.

And when, before my departure from Russia, I sold it to a Tartar man, I sold part of my soul—and all my youth.

O blissful spring, not of this world...
That was how Pavlik's poem—which I heard God knows when—an eternity ago!—in a dark train car from someone, who was killed and buried long ago—echoed in the three of us:

> O blissful spring, not of this world,
> Carried by—Mozart and Rossetti...[73]
> A toy—a chatter—a flower—an anachronism—
> An aimless spring—whose name is—Romanticism.

---

[73] Dante Gabriel Rossetti (1828–1882), a British poet, illustrator, painter, and translator.

How long did they last these jointly sleepless nights of ours? In feeling—an eternity, but, in the same feeling: only one endless, fast-flowing night. Strangely, it was not a black night, nor a moon-lit one—even though it probably was black, or perhaps there was a moon—and not a blue one from the lamppost, which *didn't* work, because by the spring all the electricity was out. It was a somewhat silver, diffused, dreamy, dawn-like night, entirely—dawn-like, with our glimmering-in-the gloom faces. Or maybe it stayed in my memory that way—because of Sonechka's words:

—Marina! I understand, you see, why it's—*White Nights*! Because I now also love—two people. But why does it feel so good? What about you, Marina?

—It's not two people, but—both, Sonechka! And I also love—both. And I too feel "so good." And you, Volodya?

—I feel (*with a deep sigh*) *good*, Marina Ivanovna!'

—Sonechka, why don't you ever wear necklaces?
—Because I don't have any, Marina.
—I thought you didn't like them.
—Oh, Marina! I'd give my soul for a necklace, a coral one.
—Do you want to hear—a fairytale about a coral necklace? Well, listen then. Her name was Undine and his Hildebrand.[74] He was a knight, and because of a stream he ended up in this cabin, where she lived with an old man and an old woman. But the stream was her uncle—Uncle Stream, and purposely flooded so widely that the knight was forced into the cabin, which the uncle then made into an island from which there was no escape. And the same stream forced an old pastor there to marry them, and Undine gets a living soul. And right away she changed: from a soulless, that is, a happy being, to an unhappy, that is, a loving one—and I'm convinced that Hildebrand right away started to love her less, even though it's not mentioned in the fairytale. And then he took her to his castle—where, loving her less and less, he soon fell in love with the Duke's daughter—Berthalda. And the three of them went to Vienna, by a boat on the Danube. Berthalda was playing on the boat, dipping

---

74 *Undine* (1811), a fairy-tale novella by Friedrich de la Motte Fouqué (1777–1843), in which Undine, a water spirit, marries a knight named Hildebrand in order to gain a soul.

her pearl necklace in the water—suddenly, a hand appeared from the water and with devilish laughter—snatched the necklace! The surface of the water around it was covered with ugly faces, and the boat almost turned over. Then the Knight became very angry, and Undine covered his mouth with her hand, begging him not to curse her on the water, since there her relatives were strong. And the Knight calmed down, and Undine bent down to the water and whispered something flatteringly to it for a long time—and suddenly took out of it: this!

—O, Marina! What is it?

—Corals, Sonechka, Undine's necklace.

These corals had been given to me as a present by my brother Andrey the day before:

"Marina! Look what I brought you!"

From his hand to the table and over its edge poured a double waterfall of huge, dark-cherry-wine, polished like children's lips, oblong, barrel-like, stone grapes.

"They were selling it in a house, and I took it for you. Even though you're blond you should wear it. There isn't another like it."

—But what is the stone?

—It's coral.

—Can they be—like that?

As it turned out—they can. And something else turned out immediately: *such things cannot be mine*. The whole evening, I was holding them in my hands, weighing, sorting, wiping, letting them touch my cheek, and touching them—with my lips—repeatedly counting them with my lips, telling them, like a rosary—the whole evening, I was saying goodbye to them, knowing that if there's a master for this luxury born under the moon, then this master is . . .

—Oh, Marina! Are those corals? So huge? So dark? Are they yours?

—No.

—That's a pity. Whose are they then?

—They're yours, Sonechka. They're for you.

And . . . not asking me again, not yet closing her half-opened-in-amazement lips—as if her words had turned to stone, she forgot everything in the world—even me, and with both her hands immediately, in deep concentration, devoutly—put them on.

This is how Cossette once took a doll from Jean Valjean:[75] silently from being full.

—Oh, Marina! Look, they come down—to my knees!

—Wait, when you're old—they'll be on the ground.

—I better *not* get old, Marina, because is it really possible for an old woman to wear—this? Marina! I've never understood the word happiness. It's a circle—the size of the sky, drawn with a thin quill, with nothing—inside. Now I myself am—happiness. I plus the corals—equals—happiness. And—the problem's solved.

Squeezing them in her hand, as if it were possible to do it in such a hand, which could fit exactly four beads, flooded and over-loaded with them, she, like a mad person: drinks? no, eats? no—she kisses them. And with strange words at such a moment, says:

—Marina! I know, you see, that—this is my last time living.

What the corals were to Sonechka—Sonechka herself was to me.

—And what happened to—Undine's necklace?

—She handed it to Berthalda—instead of the *other one*, but the Knight grabbed it from her hands and threw it into the water and cursed Undine and her whole family... And Undine couldn't stay in the boat any longer... No, the end is too sad, Sonechka, you'll cry... But know that this necklace is—the same one, the Danube one, taken from the Danube and returned there, the necklace of overcome jealousy and posthumous faithfulness, Sonechka... and of male gratitude.

From these corals a farewell started. The corals themselves were—a farewell. Don't give your beloved something too beautiful, because the hand that gave and the hand that took will inevitably part, as if they'd already parted—in this gesture of giving and taking, this gesture of separating and not joining: empty hands—on one side, full hands—on the other. They'll inevitably part,

---

75   In Victor Hugo, *Les Misérables* (1862).

and in the gap created by the gesture of giving and taking, a whole expanse will enter.

From one hand to another—you pass on the separation, pour it, in such corals!

You see, we give such "corals"—instead of ourselves, from the impossibility of giving—ourselves, as a compensation for ourselves; through such corals, we take ourselves away—from the other. In such a present, there is treachery. No wonder that some who are prophetic at heart—fear it: "What are you taking from me—since you're giving me that?" Such corals are—a payment. In the same way, a pineapple is brought to a dying person, so as not to have to go with him into the black pit. In the same way roses are brought to a convict, so as not to have to go to Siberia with him.

—Marina! I'm going away with the Studio.

—Yes? For how many days? To perform someplace?

—Far away, Marina, for the whole summer.

"The whole summer," when you love, is a whole lifetime.

Since such presents were always given at a parting: a departure, a wedding, a birthday (it's the same farewell: to a certain year of your beloved as to a certain year of your love)—they, loaded with such meaning, start by themselves to bring on—the separation: changing gradually from accompanying it to its symbol, later its signal, and then, as the live summons: they themselves become the separation.

Maybe—if I hadn't given Sonechka those corals . . .

―――――――

Fifteen years later, walking in Paris on Rue Du Bac, somewhere in a poor corner antique shop window—I saw them. It was a blow directly to my heart: because from the corals, from the velvet stand where they were placed—suddenly the little stem of a neck and a small, rosy pink, dark-eyed face, and lips of a matching color, dark-cherry-wine, with the same strips of light as on the stones.

It was—a momentary vision. I looked again at—the dark-green velvety neck-stand with a price tag on it: a four-digit number.

―――――――

After the corals flowed the dresses, a faille one and a satin one. It happened this way. We walked by the dark hallway to the exit, and suddenly it dawned on me:

—Sonechka, stop, don't move!

Diving down, into the blackness of a huge wardrobe room that is under my feet, I immediately find myself in the time of seventy—and seven years ago, not seventy-seven, but seventy and seven—in seventy and in seven. Groping—with dreamy-infallible knowledge—for something that long ago, and deliberately under its own weight, fell, guttered, melted, collapsed, stretched itself, overflowed—in a whole metallic puddle of silk that I pour over my shoulders.

—Sonechka! Hold this!

—Oh, what is it Marina?

—Wait, wait!

And a new dive to the black bottom, and again my hand is in the puddle, but now not in the metallic one, but a mercury one—with water, running away, playing under my hands, not gathering into my palm but spreading out, flying in different directions from under my grabbing fingers, because if the first one—due to its weight, collapsed, the second—due to its lightness—flew away from the hanger—as from a branch.

And after the first, the guttering one, the brown faille one—which belonged to my great-grandmother the Countess Ledokhovsky—which was unfinished by her, unfinished by—her daughter—my grandmother—Maria Lukinichna Bernatzky, unfinished by *her* daughter, my mother, Maria Alexandrovna Mein—but made into a dress by her great-grand-daughter—the first of our Polish kin to be called "Marina"—me, in my maidenhood of seven-years-ago, but by *its cut*—belonging to my great-grandmother: the bodice like a cape and the skirt like a sea.

—And now, Sonechka, hold on!

And on the already stooped Sonechka, yielding under the weight of four female generations—on top of the brown one—there was the blue one: the blue and scarlet one, azure and wild, the Turkish one, the merchant's one, the scarlet-flower one,[76] which was in itself—a flower.

---

76 *The Scarlet Flower* by Sergey Aksakov, an adaptation of the traditional fairytale *Beauty and the Beast*.

"Marina!"—Sonechka said, staggering, not quite understanding or seeing the azure of the second one, the horse-chestnut color of the first one, because the wardrobe is—a grotto, and the hallway—a coffin... (Oh, the dark places of all my houses—past, present, and future... Oh, dark houses!... Isn't it from you comes my poetic darkness?—*Ich glaube an Nächte!*[77])

I push Sonechka in front of me like a statue on wheels, stupefied, and completely hidden under the dresses, through the utter darkness of the hallway to the semi-darkness of the dining room: the ceiling light, which used to illuminate it, hadn't been cleaned for two years, and had now changed to *that* semi-light of the dining room—from the dining room, by another dark hallway—by the dark gorge of chests and the black sea of the grand piano—to Alya's nursery—to light—finally!

I put her, wobbly and confused by the dark places, and silent as a coffin, in front of a huge, up-to-the-ceiling mirror:

—Try it on!

She blinks, as if from sleep, quickly, quickly flickers her black eyelashes, whether she'll laugh or cry is unclear:

—These are—the dresses, Sonechka. Try then on!

And here was—a momentary apparition—of white and poverty: a white neckline and poor lace: a flounce of skirt, an inset of slip—and a moment of complete disappearance under a huge bell skirt—and—in the greenish water of the sunrise mirror: in the double green of sunrise and mirror—a different apparition: a girl, a great-grandmother of a hundred years ago.

She stands, intently buttoning the twelve little buttons on all the details of its close-fitting bodice, smooths and straightens the smallest gatherings by the belt, following them with her hand to the huge waves of the hem...

I catch in her eyes—happiness—no, not happiness, but the frightened childish mortal seriousness—of a girl in front of a mirror. A gaze—of deepest inquisitiveness, checking all the gifts bestowed (and not bestowed!), the gaze of a Columbus, an Archimedes, a Nansen.[78] A gaze that lasts, what—an hour?

And finally:

—It's splen-did, Marina! Just a little too long.

---

77   "I believe in nights!" From Reiner Maria Rilke, "You darkness from which I come."
78   Fridtjof Nansen (1861–1930), a Norwegian explorer, scientist, diplomat, humanitarian, and Nobel Peace Prize laureate.

(It was—very long, so long that the prows of the ill-fated "bityugs"[79]—couldn't be seen!)

She stands, already happy, burning hot, bowing to herself in the mirror, in the mirror—to herself. After taking three steps away, while slightly lifting the sides of the gown, which was standing under its own weight—she gives a deep great-grandmother's maidenly curtsy.

—But this dress is—a ball, Marina! I'm already—swimming! I'm not moving, but the dress is *already* swimming! It—dances a waltz, Marina! No—a minuet! And will you let me wear it?

—What do you think?

—You will, you will! And I'll stand in it behind the back of my chair—how poor I looked with that chair, Marina!—but even the dress isn't—rich it's—noble, it's the one belonging to her grandmother in which Nasten'ka[80] went to hear *The Barber of Seville*! (I'll have to mention it!) Will you give it to me for tonight? Because I'll have to raise the hem.

—For today—for tomorrow—and forever.

—Whaa-at? This is—for me? But this is already heaven, Marina, such things are—simply a dream. You wouldn't believe it, Marina, but this is my first silk dress: before, I was too young, then Daddy died, then—Revolution ... I did have silk blouses, but a dress—never. (*Pause.*) Marina! When I die, you'll lay me out in this brown one. Because it was—my first such happiness ... I always thought that I loved white, but now I see that it was unintelligent. And poverty. Because there wasn't anything else. And that one—fit my color, my *stripe*, as you say. As if I were thrown into a pot as a whole: with my eyes, hair, cheeks, and it boiled and I turned out—like that. And do you think, Marina, that if I, for example, get married this summer in the provinces—I know that I *won't*, but if—I do, can I go to church in—the blue dress? Because—I was told that—now one can get married in the church even in a soldier's uniform—I mean the brides. And suppose one were getting married in jodhpurs, that is—one wanted to get married in them, but the Pope refused, and then the bride refused—to get married in church.

It's all decided, Marina! I'll get married—in the blue one, and will lie in my coffin—in the chocolate one!

---

79 Sonechka's rough shoes.
80 A character in Dostoevsky, *White Nights*.

After the dresses, it was—the yellow chest.

When I found out that she was going away, I was practically never apart from her—I took Alya to her in the morning and was with her for the rest of her life there. (And somewhere from the aural depths came the word: *règne*. Canada, where even to this day instead of *vie* they say *règne*,[81] even about some poor, insignificant human life, about the life of a lumberjack or rafts' man—*règne. Mon règne. Ton règne.* So, in French-Canadian, the remainder of Sonechka's life here, in keeping with all the rest, would be a *règne, la fin de son règne*. So I can't be accused of—hyperbole.

(For a *great* people speak of life *that* way.)

—Well, Marina, I'm packing today!

I sit on the windowsill. The green chair is—empty: Sonechka lays out and packs her things, carrying them from one place to another, like a cat with her kittens. Some sort of little cloths, little pieces of paper, little boxes ... She opens the yellow chest. And I come closer—to see her dowry at last.

The yellow chest is—empty: except for on the bottom there are new, blindingly orange children's boots.

—Sonechka? Where is the dowry?

She, holding in each hand a huge boot, which seemed even bigger—in her hand, replied:

—Here! I bought them myself—they happened to be selling them in the Studio, they belonged to someone's sister or brother. And I bought them, convincing myself that it's very practical, because they're so thick ... But no, Marina, I can't wear them: they're too hard, and again with snouts, with impudent snouts, new snouts, shiny snouts! And enough for the rest of my life! Till the grave! Now I'm selling them.

A few days later:

—So, Sonechka, did you sell the boots?

—No, Marina, I was told that it's very simple: you go there and stand—they'll grab them right away, along with your hands. And they truly were grabbing them along with my hands, but Marina, it was such torture: such stupid jokes, such obnoxious peasant women, such grim peasant men, and right away they start disparaging them, the soles are cardboard, or they are not made of leather but of one of those "raw materials" of theirs ... I started to cry—and left—and will never sell anything at Smolensky Market.

---

81   Reign. *Vie* means Life.

And the day after, to my same question, she replied:

—Oh, Marina! I'm so happy! I just gave them as a gift! To the landlord's little girl—there was such happiness! She's twelve and they're her size. I thought of them—for Alechka, but Alechka will have to wait six more whole years—for such muzzles, which might even make her cry! But the landlord's daughter, Man'ka, is—happy, because she's got legs like that—like muzzles.

In one of her pre-departure days, I found a huge young soldier at her place, delicately sitting on the edge of a piqué blanket, with his huge hands spread on his khaki knees like—lobsters:[82]

—And this, Marina, is my student, Senya. I teach him reading.

—And is it going well?

—Excellently. He's awfully sharp—right, Senya?

—It depends, Sophia Evgenevna...

—Is he reading by syllables already or only letters for now?

—Senya! (*Sonechka, blushing*)—this citizen's name is Marina Ivanovna, the famous writer—Marina Tsvetaeva. Senya, please remember it!—Marina Ivanovna thought I was teaching you to *read* the alphabet! I'm teaching him reading, expressive reading... And we are a lo-ong time literate, right, Senya?

—Second year, Sophia Evgenevna.

I'll never forget that glance of deepest admiration with which the soldier marked this "we are."

—"Comrade, comrade..." But nobody on the street calls me comrade, and almost never—citizeness, always—little citizen-wench—and right away they add something that rhymes with it. Little citizen-wench—dark like a mensch (even though I'm not at all dark, just the blush makes me look darker)—or: my darling wench. And one even made up a whole poem:

> My dear little citizen-wench
> Sit with me on this bench
> And share my bagel lunch.

---

82 A play on words: *rooki* (hands), *raki* (lobsters).

And I said to him: "And where is the bagel lunch you promised? Give it to me!"—"But I only added that so it'll rhyme, my little citizen-wench. Alas I've no little bagel lunch, because Kolchak-the-swine starves us. But if the times were different—I'd not only give you a bagel lunch, I'd drive a whole heard of sheep for you[83]—for your beautiful little eyes. Because your little eyes, my dear citizen-wench..." And it's always eyes, those eyes. Are they really so—special? And why do only soldiers like me, and doormen, and in general old ones, and never, never—intellectuals?

I've described her drawling "Marina" many times—Oh, Mari–ina, Ah, Mari-ina! But she had another "Marina," an abrupt one, with a quiver of her upper lip, which inevitably prefaced something funny: "Mr'na (something like French, "Marne") did you notice when you said, how he..." My name then was a vibration of laughter, already part of laughter, so to speak, an opening of a roulade, with letters—bubbling under the lip.

With my name she sang, complained, repented, languished, and also—laughed.

On the eve of her departure she brought a present for Alya: *Childhood and Adolescence*, in a red binding, her own children's one with the blue eyes of Seryozha Ivin[84] and his battered knee, and a whole page of tender dedications.

—Oh, Marina! How much I wanted to give you my *Netochka Nezvanova*,[85] but it was stolen from me, taken and never given back. Marina! If you ever see it—buy it for yourself from me as a keepsake. In it is all of me to you, because this story is about us, and it is unfinished—just like ours...

Then there was a last evening, a last gramophone, a last of the three of us, a last departure—into a last sunrise.

---

83 Another play on words: *baranka* (little bagel), *baran* (sheep).
84 A character in Tolstoy, *Childhood and Adolescence*.
85 An unfinished novel by Dostoevsky.

An empty square—in front of which train station? It seems to me—in front of a God-forsaken one. I don't know—maybe Bryansky—a wooden one perhaps. Peasant men, bags. Peasant women, bags. Soldiers, bags. And still—empty. A perpendicular sun, an azure sky—the blue of that dress.

Standing there—Sonechka, that soldier, and I.

—And this, Marina, is my female pupil!

Toward us—swallowing a dozen paving stones at once with her feet, came—a female colossus, a maiden colossus, with a light-brown braid as thick as a fist, in a blue skirt down to her knees, from which to the ground was more than a good half-fathom, with cheeks of red varnish, of such red and such varnish that Sonechka's seemed pale.

And Sonechka, in response to my astonished gaze, said:

—Yes, and we are only sixteen years old. And it is our first year after leaving the village. We want to be on the stage. That's the kind of miracle that exists in our Russia!

And rising on her tiptoes, she lovingly pets her. And the female pupil, against all probability, reddens even more, and in a mighty bass says:

—Sophia Evgenevna, I brought you provisions for the journey. (*Taking out a mighty bag.*) The whole month—you'll be full.

The platform. Sonechka, already inside, cries tears from the car directly onto the platform:

—Marina! Marina! Marina! Marina!

I, not knowing how to console her:

—Sonechka! There will be a river there! And nuts!

—What are you taking me for, Marina, a soulless squirrel? (*Crying.*) Without you, Marina, a nut isn't a nut for me!

... Kiss—Alechka!

... Kiss—my gramophone!

... Kiss—Volodechka!

Letter 1

My precious Marina!

I couldn't hold back my tears—and cried while walking on Povarskaya Street, which was so bright this morning. It will happen again and again. I'll see you not once, and I'll cry not once, but not like *this*—never, never—

I'm endlessly grateful for every minute I was with you and I'm sorry about those I gave to the others—seeeriously, I'm very much asking forgiveness that I once told Volodya—that he was the dearest.

—The dearest is—you, my Marina.

If I don't die, and will want again—an autumn, a season, a theater—it will only be due to your love, and I'd die without it—or more exactly—without you. Because to know that you—exist is to know that there's no—Death. And will Volodya with his strong arms be able to seize me away from Death?

I kiss your hands a thousand times, the ones that should just be kissed, but they—move cupboards and lift heavy things—how immeasurably I love them for it.

I don't know what else to say—I've a thousand words—but I need to leave. Farewell, Marina—remember me—I know that I'll torture myself with memories of you for the whole summer—Marina, Marina, such a dear name—to whom will I say it?

On the eternal and endless Journey—

Your

Sonya Holliday (I like my last name—because of Irina, my little girl).

Letter 2

My things are packed.—My life, farewell!—How many mornings I greeted in my green chair—alone with thoughts of you. I love everything here—because you were here. I'm leaving with pain—for the same reason.

Marina—my dear, my beautiful—I can't write, all I do is cry so foolishly. My heart—farewell.

Your Sonya.

Letter 3

(*For Alya*)

I kiss you—I kiss your little thin arms which used to embrace me—good-bye, my dear Alya—will we see one another again?

Cast a spell to bring about happiness and Big Love—for small and not very happy me.

Your Sonya.

Letter 4

June 20 (June 7, old calendar) 1919.

My dear Marina—my heart—I live in immeasurable chaos—everyone is whistling, singing, squealing, giggling. I can't collect my thoughts—but in my heart I know about my love for you, which I walk around with all my days and nights.

I'm not good now, Marina, and I don't rejoice in the marvelous air, in the forest and larks—Marina, I can only know, feel, and understand it all, when you, Volodya, my Yurochka—and even the gramophone—are with me—I'm not even talking about Chopin and "The Twelfth Rhapsody"—when *He* is with me, whom I don't yet know and whom I'll never meet.

I can live with my pulse beating 150 after even a fleeting glance—one can't prohibit the eyes from smiling!—but here I'm alone—and though the village girls adore me, I'm as lonely as the telegraph poles along the railway line. Yesterday, I walked for a long time by myself in the direction of Moscow and thought: how the poles, lonely things, are heartsick—even the telegrams don't pass in them! Marina, I'll describe an empty incident to you, but you'll laugh and understand why I'm heartsick today.

Yesterday, I sat at Evgeny Bagartionovich's and led a joking dialog with a peasant woman:

The woman: Who, my beauty, are you filling up the cigarettes for? For your dear husband?

Sonya: Yes.

Woman: The one in the white pants?

Sonya: Yes.

Woman: But why don't you live with him in the same hut?

Sonya: Well, he kicked me out. He said, I grew ugly—so he told me to fill up the cigarettes—so that's why I'm here, and he's taken another one.

The evening of the same day, the peasant woman catches Vakhtangov and says:

—Why did you leave your wife and exchange her for another one? You see, your wife's a beauty. And you took this one? Aren't you ashamed? Live with your wife!

The night of the same day.

I'm washing my face in the hallway and Vakhtangov comes in:

—Sophia Evgenevna what are you, a child or an adventuress, with your story to the woman?

I ran away from Vakhtangov and I'm madly sorry that I'm not with him.

This is all empty—Marina, please write to me, my joy—please, write. Starting tomorrow I'm moving into a separate room and will write a journal for you, my dear. —Write to me, I beg you. I don't understand how I live without you...

Write letters to G-r[86]—and let Volodya read them too.—How is he?

Marina, they're taking my things—I have to send the letter—don't forget me. I'm asking, begging—write to me.

Oh, how I cried while reading your last letter, how much I love you.—I kiss your precious hands, your oblong, strict eyes, and—if only I could kiss it—your enchantingly light voice.

I live waiting for your letters. Kiss Alechka and Irina. My gramophone—where is it all?

Your S.

Letter 5
(The last one)

July 1 (June 20 old calendar) 1919.

Jerkwater little city, Shishkeev.

—Marina—do you feel by its name—where I am?!—Jerkwater city Shishkeev—wretched houses, huts, poor and dirty, and a forest so hopelessly far away that I, during these two weeks, didn't even make it there once.—I'm sad, and in the evening my soul is so torn apart with heartsickness that it always seems to me that I won't make it to the morning.

In the evenings, I used to write in my journal, but now the candle is finished, and I sit in the darkness for a long time and think about you, my dear

---

86 Lev Vladimirovich Goldenweiser (1883–1959), a Russian playwright and theater director.

Marina.—Such an unexpected joy—your letter.—My God, I cried and kissed it, and kiss your dear hands that wrote it.

—Marina, when I die, write this poem of yours on my cross.

> ... So, it ended with a refrain:
> Oh, my little one![87]

—Such an astounding poem.

—Marina, my heart, I'm writing so disconnectedly. It's daytime now, the bluest and hottest time—everything's so noisy that I can't think.—I write in a mad hurry, since Vakhtang Levanovich is going to Moscow—and I have only thirty minutes. Marina, I implore you, my heart, my Life—Marina!—don't leave for the Crimea yet, till the first of August! I'm coming back by the first. I'll die if I don't see you—I'll have nothing to live for, if I don't even see you.

—Marina, my beloved, my precious, don't leave—I don't know what else to say. I love you more than anyone, anything—it doesn't matter what else I say—through all of it.

—Marina, darling, tender, dear, I kiss you, your eyes, your hands, I kiss Alechka and her little hands for her letter. I despise the father, the son and his unintelligent love for "some married countess"—I'm upset that Volodya doesn't write, truly upset.

My heart, Marina, don't forget me.

Your Sonya.

I'm writing a journal for you.

Along the road to Ruzayevka, from one of the stations, I sent a telegram to Volodya:

> I kiss you—across the hundreds of
> miles separating us![88]

I gave it to the telegraph clerk, but he didn't want to take such a telegram as an urgent one—saying, "It's not right." I barely prevailed on him.

Kisses.

I'm praying for you.

---

87 From the cycle of *Poems to Sonechka* (1919).

88 A line from "No one was left at a loss," a poem that Tsvetaeva wrote to Osip Mandelstam.

Sonya.

P.S. Across from my house there's a church, I go there for matins and cry.

———————

After Sonechka's departure, I faint-heartedly began to assemble her from the tracks she left. It suddenly seemed to me—I suddenly ordered myself to believe—that she was nothing special, that in her circle—everyone was like that.

But, to my surprise, I soon realized that Sonechka was somehow—so to speak—not there, just like when someone who lacks cigarettes automatically puts in his mouth—something long: a pencil—or a toothbrush—and it calms him down for a while, but afterward he notices that because of his previous distress he picked up—the wrong thing.

The students accepted me, heartily, famously, when I followed the tracks of Sonechka's love, one female student even offered to take Irina to some other village when she returned . . . We met a few times—but—she was fair-haired and blue-eyed and soon I realized that it had nothing to do with Sonechka. The girl was—my acquaintance. My new strange acquaintance.

As in a book with—"to be continued," here it's—"not to be continued."

———————

It was, though, to be continued—with Volodya, our continuation, the continuation of the previous us, the pre-Sonechka, not-separated, and not-brought-together-by-her, us. After the disappearance of her little physical presence between us, it might have seemed natural to fill in the little physical absence, to fill it in with ourselves, by slightly moving toward one another, to simply sit side by side, to find ourselves alongside. But no—as if by an agreement—but without an agreement—with her disappearance from between us—we moved apart, he to his faraway corner, I—to my faraway corner, a whole good one-and-a-half Sonechka-lengths away from one another. The vanished little black head between us didn't bring our heads closer. As if that thing with Sonechka was just dreamt of and possible only with her: only in a dream.

But here should sound the name, *Martin Eden*.[89]

---

89   An autobiographical novel published in 1909 by the American writer Jack London.

—This is—more than words can say: a work, a hero, an author. More than *I* can say... Someday, when we separate... —Marina Ivanovna, please, read *Martin Eden*, and when you come to the place with the curly fair-haired horseman on the white horse remember and understand me.

Nineteen years later, nineteen-and-a half years later, in November 1937, I was walking in Paris in the rain along an unfamiliar little street with a Russian companion, Kolya—who was a bit older than Volodya was then.

—Marina Ivanovna! Here are some old books—in the rain—maybe you want to take a look?

I open the tarpaulin: Martin Eden looks at me with his eyes.

Now—an explanation. It would be wild to think that I, who live only by dream and memory—forgot that request of Volodya's.

But—simply to walk into a shop and ask for *Martin Eden*?

The same way that one day Volodya came into my life—on his own, like everything else big in my life—or didn't come at all, that's how Martin Eden had to come.

And so, he came—today, in the rain, because of the chance word of my traveling companion.

So, he appeared.

All I had to do was—stretch out my hand: to him, drowning in the rain and perishing from the indifference of the passers-by. (Let's remember the end of Martin Eden and of Jack London himself!)

To buy in a thriving shop—a new, not yet cut *Martin Eden*, any *Martin Eden*, the next copy of *Martin Eden*—would be a betrayal of Volodya himself, a triple betrayal: of Jack London, Martin Eden, and Volodya. It would be the triumph of *la chose établie*,[90] which all three of them gave their lives fighting against.

And this way—in the rain—from under the tarpaulin—in the last minute before closing—from the hands of an indifferent saleswoman—it was simply a case of saving: Martin Eden and a memory of Volodya himself. Here Martin Eden needed me. Here I was stretching out my helping hand to him, here, truly with my hand, I—came to his aid.

And there, at the end of this immortal book—oh, I wasn't looking for that fair-haired horseman, and wasn't even waiting for him, knowing that he'd appear—in his own time, on his own line!—at the end of this hymn to lonely

---

90 The established order.

labor and growth, this hymn to *solitude*, in what was already his final hour in the world—came...

—a vision of white, not a horseman, but a rower, a swimmer, a Pacific white savage standing on a split,[91] in whom I recognized the fair-haired horseman—who never existed except in my memory.

Nineteen years later *Martin Eden*—confirmed Volodya for me.

Once I was reading to him from my notebook—about Z-sky, Pavlik, Sonechka, myself, talks in waiting lines, thoughts, and so on—and he, with some joking bitterness said:

—Marina Ivanovna, it's somehow upsetting to me—why is there nothing about me? about—us? about—our relationship?... You understand, that in the outer world, in life, I'm not at all jealous, but rather in the world of thoughts—or what shall I call it? I, myself, never write anything down—even my handwriting is childish—I know that everything is—eternal, in me eternal, and that everything stays and at the right moment—appears, everything, every word of ours. I even have a feeling that I, by writing something—would insult, belittle it... But you—you're different, you're a writer...

—And did you ever notice this, even once during our whole friendship, Volodya?

—(*He, grinning:*) The others said...

—Wait, Volodya! I do have something about you—two lines, the end of a poem, which was never finished:

> If God made you his anointed King
> People would name you—"the Quietest."

I see with my own eyes how he lets the poem enter his breast and listens to it there. And with the start of another grin he says:

—Marina Ivanovna, it's only with you that I'm so quiet.

I haven't said anything yet about his smile, which was: rare, short, shy, self-embarrassed, from under unchangeably down-cast eyes—those—indulgent and even condescending eyes, with which he looked at me, or rather didn't

---

91 No split is in fact mentioned in the closing scene of *Martin Eden*.

look at me, when I started talking about Z-sky. A smile with almost forcefully brought together lips, brought back to their previous place of non-laughter. Strange but true, and I'm asking you to check this, such a smile happens to— two-year-olds, children who as yet talk little, accompanied by fixed, averted, sometimes squeezed shut—eyes. Yes, Volodya had a *childlike* smile, if you exclude all the commonplaces connected to children's ones . . .

Moreover—such a smile (of hidden triumph and obvious embarrassment) appears on the faces of very young fathers—at their first-born: certainly at—a son. And if in the forcefully brought together lips there was embarrassment, in the eyes there was—superiority.

Volodya, Volodya—when somewhere, on someone's face, either— a two-year-old child in a public garden, or a forty-year-old English captain in a film—I see the *beginning* of such a smile—the public garden, the film, the child, the captain all disappear, and the smile ends up—being yours.

And everything is—just as it was then.

We never spoke about Sonechka. I knew he loved her differently than I did, and that she loved him differently than she did me, that we wouldn't sing the same song, that for him she was—less than she was, because with him she was—less, because everything that she was—she was with me, and to be everything with two separate people is impossible. It's possible only with two at the same time, which is how it was with the three of us in our triangle, till it—ended.

I don't even know if he wrote to her.

A conversation about her would definitely be an argument. I felt that he didn't have—the key to her, and to say it all: he was too young, too young for her childishness, so that he, with his twenty years, couldn't feel the whole of her misfortune and fate. For him to love was—to worship, and how could one worship a little one—than whom, even on your knees, you will unavoidably be—taller and older?

And our gramophone, which turned out to be only Sonechka's voice, fell silent, that second synchronous voice at the absence of which in her breast she so often and arduously complained.

Sonechka, with her gramophone, her green chair, her rusty-red unsold shoes, her Yura, her Volodya, even with her me, with everything of hers and all of herself, re-settled entirely in my heart, and I—with her in my heart—

entirely moved into the future, to the day of our meeting, in which I had deep faith.

All these days without her were—as if I had been standing, shading my eyes from the sun with my hand, like a peasant woman in a field—is she coming? Or slept like a girl who was promised a new doll—and here she is still asleep, asleep, asleep, and gets up—sleeps, and goes to bed—sleeps—waiting for the time to pass! Or—like a prisoner who daily crosses off one more mark on the wall. Like walking to meet someone—I lived to meet her, I walked to meet her—with every footstep, and in every moment of the day, and every thought in my head—just like her, along the tracks in the direction of Moscow, that is—toward me.

Oh, I was never longing for her—I was rejoicing in her too much!

Here are her echoes—in my notebook of those days:[92]

"Now in front of me are Alya's knees and her long legs. She lies on the roof, with her legs down the skylight:—Marina! There's a cloud floating by—maybe it's your mother's soul? Marina, maybe now the Little Mermaid is coming to our house, the one who was three hundred years old? (*And she crosses herself when she hears the music from the street.*)—Marina! Marina! Marina! How the smoke flies.—My God! This smoke is flying everywhere, everywhere! Marina, maybe it's smoke from the train Sonechka is on?—Marina, maybe this smoke is from Joan of Arc's stake? And there are so many souls at this height, aren't there?"

... "I won't talk about the women, because I remember them all with gratitude, but I love only Sonechka Holliday."

"When I think about Sonechka Holliday's arrival, I don't believe it: there couldn't be such happiness.

I think about her—while skipping the main thing—like about a new ring, a pink dress—I know it sounds funny: with desire. Because it's not Sonechka's coming—but Love itself.

I dream about Sonechka Holliday, like about a lump of sugar: a *guaranteed*—sweetness."

---

92   From Tsvetaeva's journal #6, 1919.

(Let this whole story be—like a lump of sugar, at least it was *sweet* to write it!)

—Marina Ivanovna! Today is our last evening. Tomorrow I'm going to the South.

—Last one... tomorrow... But why didn't you... you could have said earlier...

—Marina Ivanovna! (*his voice was serious—even warning*) Don't make me tell you something that isn't necessary: for me—to say, or for you—to hear. You may be sure that I had—very good reasons.

—To hide the end—from me? Visiting me as if nothing at all was happening? Yet knowing? You alone knowing?

—Well, if you really want to know...

—Neither really nor not really, I simply—want nothing, and God be with you in everything! I simply—dreamt all this—the extra time—I dreamt *all* this!

—Marina Ivanovna! Nevertheless, you're—human and I'm—human too, and to be human is—to feel pain. Why then should I, to whom you gave so much joy, only joy, give you this pain—and before its time? Mine was—enough.

—Volodya, is this your final decision?

—My suitcase is already packed.

—Are you going on your own?

—No, there are a few of us. A few—from the Studio. And then later I'll separate from them.

—Am I understanding you correctly?

—Yes.—And what about your parents?

—They think—I'm going to act. Everyone thinks—it's to act. Only you—know. Marina Ivanovna, I've nothing to do here anymore. There's no life—here. Here *for me*—no life. I can't play life, when others—live it. To play when others are—dying. I'm not an actor.

—This, I—always knew.

—And now let's forget it and spend the evening as usual.

And we spent the evening—as usual. And it *passed*—like any evening.

At one moment with him, I felt—as if a veil fell from my eyes!

—But the Angel was you, Volodechka![93]

—What? (*and, after he understood, shyly:*) Ah, you mean about this . . . ? (*And then, firmly:*)—No, Marina Ivanovna, I'm no angel. My biggest dream is: to become a human one day.

And then in a tone that wasn't his, in Sonechka's sleepy, dreamy, self-addressing, not to me, voice:

—Maybe, I was too honest . . .

And later again:

—Charlemagne—or maybe *not* Charlemagne—said: "With God one should speak Latin, with the enemy—German, with a woman—French . . ." (*Silence*)—And here—it sometimes seems to me—that I speak Latin with women . . .

(I didn't hug him . . . that wasn't what he wanted from me—or for himself with me . . .)

Right before his departure, still in the room—already almost light:

—Marina Ivanovna, you always liked this ring. Take it! I wanted to give it to you from the first moment, and since then, at almost every meeting. But I was—waiting—for something. Now it has come. This isn't a present, Marina Ivanovna, it's—a tribute.

—Volodya! It seems that this is the first ring ever given to *me*. It's always—I who gives. (*I take mine off and hold it.*) If I haven't yet given one to you, it's only because I've already given one to Yury Z. and Pavlik, and to many others—before them! I didn't want, I couldn't stand, that you would—somehow—be put in the same row.

—And *how* envious I was of them, now I can tell you, and of Pavlik, and of Z-sky—that it was from *your* hand—and such an inalterable thing! Honestly (*laughing*)—I burned with envy! No, Marina Ivanovna, you'll certainly give it to me—I won't be put in the same row by it, if I stayed in the Studio—

---

93 A reference to Tsvetaeva's play *The Stone Angel*.

I'd be in the same row, but there, where I'm going . . . And even to be in the same row—in *that* row, isn't an insult.

Now admiring it:

—And the signet's empty for a name. I'm so used to seeing it on your hand that now my own hand seems to be yours. (*Holding it on an outstretched hand.*) And Z-sky's one is—smaller. Z-sky's is—from a Chinese woman, but mine is—from a Chinese man—from a Chinese sage.

—It's from a simple coolie, Volodechka.

—And if in addition he's a coolie . . . the whole social question is solved!

We're joking, joking, and the heartsickness is growing, growing . . .

—Volodya, do you know why poets exist? So it won't be embarrassing to say—the very biggest things:

> And will my paths always preserve
> —your signet.[94]

We stand under my elm trees, which some time ago were barely green, and now are silver—so silver that one couldn't see the branches or trunk.

—No, no, Marina Ivanovna, don't think that, it's not yet our last time. I'll come tomorrow too, that is, today—already today. I'll come today one more time—for the children's photos, and to say a final farewell.

When he came on "the next day" and, for the first time seeing him—in the daylight and even in the sun, after our already-a-century ago first and only day walk, I was simply stunned:

—Volodya! What is this? You aren't at all black-haired? You're—light brown-haired!

—And even lighter then light brown, Marina Ivanovna.

—Dear God, and I for the whole year-and-half was friends with the black-haired one!

—You'd probably even say that my eyes are—black? (*said with a bit of sorrow*).

—No, blue-greyish, that I always knew, and was friends with—the grey ones. But that hair is—a dream of some sort!

---

[94] Slightly changed lines from Max Voloshin (see note 15 in Autobiography, below), "Now I'm dead."

—Marina Ivanovna, I'm afraid (*in his voice under the guise of a joke is obvious bitterness*) that you saw all the rest of me in your own way! The whole of me—and not only (*with a contemptuous gesture to his hair*) this!

—And *if* so—did I see badly?

—No, Marina Ivanovna, you saw well, even very well. That's why—with you—I'm afraid of the daylight. Here, I've already turned out to be light brown-haired, and tomorrow I could turn out to be—boring. Maybe it's—good that I'm leaving?

—Volodya! Don't try my patience, my last patience with you, our last patience! Because you won't be happy yourself—and also maybe you won't leave! I've got a mouth full, understand, a mouth full—and now I'll suffocate—with all of it.

—No, *don't*, Marina Ivanova.

We sit now in that attic room from which Alya was climbing to meet me on the roof:

Alechka! I've a favor to ask: read your Mama's poems to me!

—Right this minute, Volodechka!

She comes back with a crimson notebook, which she keeps under the pillow in the kitchen.

> Your gray donkey walks straight onward
> He's not afraid of river or abyss...
> My beloved Christmas Lady,
> Take me with you—to the clouds' bliss!
>
> I'll find some bread for the little donkey...[95]

Her little voice is murmuring...

—Marina Ivanovna, I brought a present for you! My favorite book—about Joan of Arc, don't you know it? By Mark Twain—a great one.

I open it. There's an inscription. Without reading—I close it.

---

95 "The Christmas Lady," published in Tsvetaeva's collection of early poems, *Magic Lantern* (1912).

—Marina Ivanovna, I always bragged—that I've got a whole armory—my museum—my library—but I haven't shown it to anyone, because all I have is: a Gishpanish pishtol, a ring, and two books: *Martin Eden*—and this one. Now you've got—my whole arsenal—my whole museum—my whole library. I'm—clean.

—Marina! (*Alya's voice*) May I give my *Magic Lantern* to Volodya? So he can read it on the train, in case the soldiers curse. He could read it to *them*, because they, in surprise, will calm down and fall asleep. Because villagers always fell asleep from poems. When I read it to Nadya, she always fell asleep.

Volodya, kissing her little hand with the book in it:

—I'm not traveling with soldiers, but with mad people, they say—quietly mad, but now there is no such thing as quietly mad—everyone is wildly mad.

—Well, *they* definitely won't fall asleep—from Marina's poems!

—(*Alya*) Volodya, Marina and I wrote letters for you to read on the way, as we did some time ago for Papa, so he could read them on the train. These are our farewell voices.

—When is your train?
—Soon. I already have to go.
—And to see you off...?
—No, Marina Ivanovna, I want to say goodbye to you—here.

—Now, let's sit down before the road.[96]

We sit in a row, on the narrow, redwood couch. Alya, praying out loud:

—God, grant Volodya good travels and to find in the South what he's looking for. And then let him return to Moscow—on a white horse. And let us still be alive and our house still standing. Amen.

We cross ourselves, get up and walk down the narrow mezzanine staircase into the eternal darkness of the hallway. In response to my perennial inclination to walk further with him:

—Don't come any further. It'll be hard to walk.

---

96 A Russian custom.

Last minute. Will I say it or not? Will he say it or—

Simply, as if he had done this all his life, he embraces my head, squeezes it to his chest, kisses it, kisses my forehead, kisses my lips.

Then I cross him three times with that main cross of his face, above his forehead, his shoulders, his chest, with the fundamental +, that of his face.

He steps off, already beyond the threshold. And across the threshold, already without a hand:

—Farewell, Marina (*and swallowing a mountain*)—Ivanovna.

Dear Volodya!

I hope it won't be stuffy on the train, and that you'll be fed there, treated well, and that nobody will bother you, and that you'll get an open window. I'd like your journey to be as good and as rapturous as before. You, our last real friend, are leaving.

Volodya! I just raised my head and was ready to burst into tears. I'm very sad. You're the last one who really loved us, you were so tender with us, you listened to the poems so well. You've got Marina's children's book. You'll read it and remember how I—read it to you. Soon someone will go to Kiev and we'll again write letters to you.

Volodya, it seems untrue that you won't be here. Oh, dear God! Let the train not be burned, because all the passengers are innocent. Please, try to be unnoticeable and make up a good illness for yourself. Maybe something terrible will happen...

These parting terrors of Alya's remain—incomplete, because right away there was Volodya's parting knock, and I didn't have enough time to write her whole letter into my notebook. I think that what followed was the description of Volodya's transfer at Kiev railway station from that mad train to—a covered wagon, as the most dangerous of all mad people.

Inscribed in the book about Joan of Arc was: You and I love—the same.

Then came one single letter with a few lines. The letter ended:

—Now I've got good hope that we'll see one another again. I'll live by this faith.

Then began—the silence.

A knock on the door. I open it—Sonechka.

Joy? No. A blow—of such force that I was barely able to stand on my feet.

And in my ears a dear flow: "Marina... (*and something else, something else, and then something else again*) Ma-rina... (*and only gradually the words stand out from the flow*)—Only an hour, only an hour, only an hour.—I've got only an hour... I've got only an hour with you! I've just come and am leaving again soon... We have only an hour! I came only for you. Only an hour!"

On the stairs we bump into tenants going down.

Sonechka:

—I'm Sophia Evgenevna Holliday. I need to say a few words to you.

(*Father and son obediently turn around and come up. We all stand on the landing:*)

—Nasty people! How can you exploit a woman, who lives alone, without a husband, with two small children?!

—Well, we... well, we...

—You break into the kitchen when she's asleep, to wash (snorting like three cats!) under the faucet! As if you'd be cleaner after it! You sell her watch and don't give her the money! In her room, where her books and notebooks are, you hang your foul dirty clothes!

—But allow me... Sophia Evgenevna? (*the young one said, touchingly*) we only hang the wet clean clothes!

—They're clean, but still foul! There's an attic with beams, but you're too lazy to climb there!

—But the floor's collapsing and the beams fall on our heads...

—Marvelous, that it's collapsing... marvelous that they fall...

—And finally, Marina Ivanovna is renting this room—to us.

—But you've never paid her.

—That's because we're out of money now: but we don't refuse...

—In a word, it's—unintelligent. Your whole conduct with Marina, un-in-tel-igent. And even criminal. When the whole courtyard was full of soldiers in the middle of the night, you didn't wake her? Didn't you push under her door some kind of idiotic memoirs and portraits and an entire Maltese sword?

—But Marina Ivanovna said herself, that in case...

—I know that she said it herself. And you use it. And what if she'd been shot? (*The father is silent and breathing heavily and noisily, while agreeing in his inner soul with everything.*)

—In a word, remember, I'm leaving now. But I'll be back. And if I find out that you . . . do you understand me? I'll bring on you—a misfortune—an illness—typhus—scabies . . . and whatever else—I'll simply *curse* you!

(I have to say that after that the Polish men calmed down and—with the first frosts—moved out. I add that they were not bad people, but that I'm—a big fool.)

We sit upstairs, on the couch of Volodya's farewell. The whole room is in an oblique sunlight—of tears.

—Marina, I feel strange—as if I've died already and am visiting places . . . —Marina, does the gramophone—still work?

—I haven't turned it on since then, Sonechka.

—And there's no Volodechka. It's not that he isn't here—he often wasn't here—but that he won't come in now . . . Only a week since he left? What a pity . . .

. . . If I'd only known that everything would be so terrible, maybe I wouldn't have come to you the first time?

Is that where the cat used to climb to you, through the hole in the window? Every night—at what time? Marina, maybe it was my death—did it smell like valerian?—when people die, you see it always smells like ether.[97] Because why would he climb, if there wasn't anything to eat? He came for me, Marina, for our death, for the end of this whole thing . . . He was so light, light grey, almost invisible, wasn't he—like a sunrise? And all covered in spit? Oh, what filth, Marina, what filth! Of course, it was *no* cat, Marina—judging by your acquiescence . . . And I didn't sleep in these hours and cried, cried terribly, Marina, for you and for me . . .

. . . Marina, if you ever hear that I have girlfriends, a girlfriend—don't believe it: it's my same eternal fear of loneliness, my awful weakness, which you never wanted to admit existed in me.

As for—a man, don't believe it. Because it's always fog—or pity—or, in general, self-forgetting.

---

97 To which valerian was added to cloak the smell.

You I loved when in my full right mind and strong memory, but nevertheless loved madly.

This, Marina, is my testament.

... I bequeath Yura to you, he isn't as worthless as he seems *even to us*, not so soulless ... I don't know if he's in town now. I only have an hour, and this hour is—yours. And I don't dare ask you ... Marina! I don't dare ask you, but I'll beg you: don't leave Yura! Sometimes at least think about him—with kindness ... And if you meet him in the winter (I, of course, will return in the fall), tell him, but not straightforwardly—he doesn't like it—well, *you'll*—know how—that even if I get married, he's still my favorite of the angels ...

And Volodya—I'd love all my life so much, love him my whole life, but he couldn't love me—he could only kiss me—and even that (*laughing a bit*) somehow reluctantly, somehow strained. That's why he kissed me so hard.

Do you have a feeling that he'll come back sometime?

... And my Alechka isn't here ... Tell her, when she returns from her Krylatsky[98] (what a marvelous name!) that I'd like a daughter like her, just like her—even though I know I'll never have one.

Why, Marina, had I to love everything of yours, everything to the last spider web in the house, to the last gap in the house? To lose—it all?

... What time is it? Ah, this is how it is in your—*Adventure*—she's always asking, "what time is it?" And then again, "what time is it?" And never hears the answer, because it's not "what time is it," but: "when is—death?" Marina, can't we get it all back, take it and turn it back—with our hands, like a river? Let it flow—backwards? So that the winter would be here again—and that stage—and you reading *Snowstorm*. So, it won't be the last time, but—the first time?

... Oh, if anyone had told me that it would all end this way, I just wouldn't have come to you for the first time, I'd have refused—to come into the world!

... But still, what time is it, Marina? Now I'm—seeerious. Because they didn't want to let me—come to you. I nearly begged. I gave them my word that I'd be at the railway station at four ...

---

98   A Moscow suburb. The word means winged.

Marina, why am I going? You see, will it kill anyone—if I don't go? No one will die. Marina, can you understand me? I'm leaving you now, who for me is—everything, just because I gave my word to be at the station at four. But at the station—for what? Who made it all happen?

No, Marina, it's not worth describing—and there's already no time. (*What time is it, Marina?*) It was—as if everywhere always was and will be without you: *nonexistent. I* didn't exist, everything didn't exist. I now (*sobbing violently*) for the first time during this whole month—I'm alive, the last hour before death—alive, and however much is left of my life, Marina—this is my last hour.

We got up, walking. Stopping on the kitchen threshold.

And my Irina isn't here. I knew she wouldn't be, but somehow didn't expect an empty little bed . . . (*to herself, with a lost expression*), Halli-dah, Halli-dah . . .

Marina, I want to go to your room—to say goodbye to the lamp, the gramophone . . . Ah, I forgot, there are now these Polish men and their wet "clean clothes."

Marina! Don't see me off! Even to the stairs! Let it all be just like the first time when I came to you: I—on that side of the threshold, you—on the other one, and that beloved face of yours—in the darkness of the hallway.

I'm going with the "second group" (*laughing through her tears*) like a convict! Son'ka-convict is what I am. I can't after being with you—be with them! I'll either kill them or jump out of the window myself! (*Quietly, almost whispering:*)

> From the evil-wee love thought
> I will leave by the railroad
> And the engine'll start puffing.
> To its sound that's so gloomy
> I'll be thinking, I'll be thinking
> That the Devil is taking me . . . [99]

Marina! How *awfully* it all comes true! Because the Devil himself is taking me from you . . .

Her last words in my ears:

—Marina! I'll be back in the fall! I'll be back in the fall!

---

99 From Tsvetaeva's cycle, *Poems to Sonechka*.

———

—So, did you see your Sonechka?

—Sonechka? When?

—What do you mean, when? Yesterday, of course, since she left yesterday. I can't believe she didn't come by? That's how unfaithful she is.

"I don't know why I suddenly pictured my room grown old... The walls and the floors looked discolored, everything had become dingy, and the spider webs were thicker than ever. I don't know why, but when I looked out the window, it seemed to me that the house across the street had grown old and dingy too, that the plaster on the columns was peeling off and cracking, that the cornices were blackened and cracked, and that the deep-yellow color of the walls had become patchy.

"Either the sunbeam that suddenly peeped out was hidden again under the rainy clouds and everything had grown dim again before my eyes, or perhaps the whole prospect of my future flashed before me so sad and forbidding, and I saw myself just as I am now, fifteen years ahead, older, in the same room, just as lonely..."[100]

———

After the first blow, which I paid for with a stony lump in my entire affected breast, a deadly cold in my heart, and an undying cold in my forehead—Caesar-like (no need to laugh!) I thought, "*Et tu, Brute?*"—in which I hear not a reproach, but—pity, and—leniency—as if Brutus were lying there, and Caesar above him—bending down...

But let's shorten it and say simply: I didn't understand, but received the information—in the way one receives a blow: because you're—a body, and this body of yours was in the way.

Up to the time of my departure from Russia—in April 1922, that is, three whole years, I didn't make a single attempt to find Sonechka. For three years of coexisting with her in the same country, I thought of her as dead: past. And this was—from the first minute of the news, from the last syllable of the phrase: "She was here and left."

"But do you imagine that I could bare you a grudge, Nasten'ka?"[101]

---

100 Dostoevsky, *White Nights*.
101 Dostoevsky, *White Nights*.

There wasn't a grudge.

I *knew* that her not coming was—an appearance, an absence—imaginary, how could someone who is accompanying you like blood in your veins *be absent*—the one who won't see the light of day without the blood from your heart?

And if I was angry at first and indignant, it was only on the surface—on the surface of this reaction, hoping to turn everything by my indignation into the usual: to avert—the fatal. (If I'm angry or upset at Sonechka—that means she—exists.)

But not for a second deep in my soul did I believe that she—for some banal reason or other—didn't come, simply didn't come—*didn't come*.

And the more people—sympathized with me: speaking of "ungratefulness," "flippancy," "inconstancy"—the more I knew. Profoundly. In solitude.

I knew we had to separate. If I'd been a man—it would have been the most happy love—but this way—we inevitably had to separate, for her love for me would inevitably be—and was already—on the way—to loving another, who'd always be a shadow, and whom she'd always betray with me, as she inevitably did Yura and Volodya.

She inevitably had to tear herself from me—from the meat of her soul, hers and mine.

Sonechka left me for her woman's destiny. Her not coming to me was only her obedience to her female lot: to love a man—in the end, it doesn't matter what kind—and to love him alone till death.

In no commandment was I—my love for her, her love for me, our love—included. About her and me there wasn't any singing in the Church or writings in the Gospels.

Her leaving me was a simple and honest fulfillment of the Apostle's word: "And a man shall leave his mother and father . . ."[102] I was to her more than father and mother, without a doubt, more than that beloved man, but she had to prefer him, the unknown one. Because this is how, while creating the world, God ordained it.

And, after all, we both went against "people": never against God and never against humankind.

---

102 Genesis 2:24.

But how to reconcile my feeling of joyful ownership of Sonechka, the materiality and inalienability, the feeling of a ring on the finger—with my releasing, freeing, letting-go arms?

Here is the answer: owning in this way would only be losing in this way. Reader, do you remember? "if anything, at one with my finger..."[103]

Sonechka was torn away from me—together with my heart.

A smart animal knows right away when death is near—here it is!—and doesn't try to heal itself with herbs. So, I, a smart animal, right away recognized—my death, and squeamish about herbs and remedies, accepted it. Not that Sonechka died for me, and not that the love died—Sonechka died out of my life, that is, she went inside, up the hill, into the cave, in which she so prophetically feared—to disappear.

You see, my whole miracle with her was—that she was outside me, and not inside, not a projection of my dreams or heartsickness, but an independent thing, outside my fantasy, outside my invention, that I didn't dream up, didn't sing, that she was not in my heart—but in my room. That for just once in my whole life I hadn't added anything, but was barely a joint-owner, that is, I received—in scope and return—a full measure.

Sonechka was given to me—to sustain—in my hands. In my arms. The fact that I held a child in my arms didn't mean that it became—mine. My hands afterward felt empty, all the same.

A mother—takes away from us each child we held. Sonechka had a mother—her fate.

Insult? Treachery?

Sonechka's not coming to me this last time was the same as Volodya's coming to me—the last time—a thing of the same weight, of the *whole* essence. It meant exactly the same thing.

---

103 See p. 16.

The way Volodya—came, she—didn't come, in the same way with her whole essence didn't come, as he—did come.

Sonechka's not coming to me was love.

It was the first step of her absence from my life, the first hour of her wordless, other-worldly presence in me, her—installation—in me.

Sonechka didn't come because she—would have died, simply cried her heart out, so that from the whole of Sonechka—there'd be only a little puddle left. Or her heart would stand still on the last syllable of my name.

Volodya came, because he couldn't separate without saying goodbye. Sonechka didn't come—because she couldn't say goodbye.

She also didn't come—in one other way: Sonechka didn't come—because she had *already* died.

Only the dead ones—don't come in that way, because they can't, because the earth is holding them. And I felt her near me for a long, long time, almost within reach of my hand, in just the same way that one feels the dead, on whose hand one can't close one's hand only because—it shouldn't be, because it would turn all the known laws upside down: equally fearing to meet the emptiness—and to meet the hand.

After all, it was only from my ears and my eyes that Sonechka disappeared.

"Give us this day our daily bread..."[104]

No, she was never for me—daily bread: who am I—that something of *that* sort could be—daily bread? This my *humilité*[105] would never allow. Not daily bread, but—a miracle, and there's no such prayer as: "Give us this day our daily miracle." In her there wasn't the heaviness of daily bread, nor the iron necessity of it, nor our being doomed to it, nothing from the "sweat of your brow"[106] . . . How could Sonechka—be earned? Even by the work of a whole life. No, something like that is only given as a gift.

Like Cordelia about—salt—from my children's book of Shakespeare's *King Lear*, the same am I about—Sonechka and sugar, with the same modesty: she was necessary for me—like sugar. As everyone knows—sugar—is not a necessity, one can live without it, and for four years of the Revolution, we did

---

104   The Lord's Prayer, Matthew 6:11.

105   Humility.

106   Genesis 3:19.

live without it, some substituting—treacle—for it, some—shredded beets, some—saccharin, some—nothing at all. Drinking unsweetened tea. No one dies of its absence. But they don't live either.

Without salt, scurvy happens, without sugar, heartsickness.

A *whole* live, white, piece of sugar—that's what Sonechka was for me.

Crude? Crude—like Cordelia: "I love according to my salt, no more, no less."[107] One can love the old King like salt . . . but a little girl? No, enough of salt. Let this be said once in the world, I loved her like sugar during the Revolution. And that's that.

> Can't you say to the moment:
> Oh, moment, stop! You are so beautiful![108]

No, this I didn't have with her. There was a different thing, contrary and larger:

> May God protect you! It would have been too beautiful.
> May God protect you! It wasn't meant to be![109]

It was a great poetic subjunctive: *if*—the soul's only poetic possession: *if*.

It was—destiny. It was Russian—"not-destined."

Let's remember the words of King David: "Seventy years are given to a human being by God, and what's beyond that is already God's mercy."

Sonechka and I were given three months, no!—the whole Sonechka, the whole three-month-eternity with her was *beyond*—human life and heart.

---

107 *Sol!* as in salary, which translates "bond."

108 Kannst Du dem Augenblicke sagen:
—Verweile noch! Du bist—so schön . . .
From Goethe, *Faust*.

109 Behüt Dich Gott!—es wär zu schön gewesen,
Behüt Dich Gott!—es hat nicht sollen sein.
From Josef Viktor von Scheffel (1826–1886), *The Trumpeter from Säckingen*.

Maria ... Miranda ... Mireille ...[110]—it was enough for her to be herself, so she could be all ...

This is how forgetful Pavlik's prophetic words came true of her:

> ... One alone—under so many names.[111]

For me—came true. But not just that the names found a face.

Every male lyric poem was previously without an object, or had a reverse object—the poet himself. For to be the *object* of the poet's whole love one must insert something into the poem, namely—oneself: one's face, as if in a mirror, which I couldn't do, since I myself wanted to love and was a poet myself. But now every male lyric—acquired for me a face: Sonechka's. All those empty spaces (you, she) that one—in any language can fill, and fill only with the overflowing of the poet's heart and the fullness of the poet's *I*, suddenly—became alive, filled with her face. In the oval emptiness, in the round zero of any women's image in the poet's poems—Sonechka's face appeared as if in a locket.

But Lenau wrote about it better: more expansively!

> The forest rages, across the sky,
> The clouds of thunder race,
> Then in the weather I espy,
> —O maiden, dear, your face![112]

All the folksongs of any nation were—about Sonechka, every savage song under the moon—about Sonechka, and Kirgiz'[113] songs—and Tahitian songs—about Sonechka, the whole of Goethe, the whole of Lenau, the whole heart-

---

110 Maria is Mary, mother of Jesus; Miranda is from Shakespeare's *The Tempest*; Mireille (as before) is from Mistral's *Mirèio*.

111 See part I, note 9.

112   *Es braust der Wald, am Himmel ziehn*
    Des Sturmes Donnerfüge,
    Da mal'ich in die Wetter hin—
    O Mädchen! Deine Züge.
Nikolaus Lenau (1802–1850), a late-romantic, Austrian writer.

113 Rugged Central Asian country on the Silk Road.

sickness of every poet—about Sonechka, all arms outstretched—to Sonechka, all separation—separation from Sonechka...

Do I need to add that after her I never loved another female creature and, of course, won't love any, because I love less and less, saving the rest of my leftover ardor for those—who won't be able to feel its warmth?

Winter of 1919–1920. Nobody knocks on the door anymore—because it doesn't lock: someone broke it. So, instead of knocking on the door there's—a stomping of boots, a shaking off of snow, and a voice from downstairs:

—Does Marina Ivanovna Tsvetaeva live here?

—Yes. Please, come up the stairs.

He comes in. A stranger. Young. I know I've never seen this person before. And also know that what has walked in is the enemy.

—I'm Alekseev, a brother of Volodya Alekseev. You don't have any news from my brother, do you?

—I had. A long time ago. One letter. Back then.

—But *we*—never got—anything.

—It was just a few words, that he hopes to meet again, that he's healthy...

—And since then?

—Nothing.

—Will you allow me to put a question to you. And, please, forgive me for it in advance. What kind relationship did you have with my brother? I'm asking you because—we were very good friends with him, everyone, the whole family—and then, last Easter—he left, went to you and (*swallowing with difficulty like Volodya*) spent his last evening—with you... Was it friendship? An affair? A liaison?

—It was love.

—How do you mean? How am I to understand you?

—As it was said. I'll—add no more.

(*He's quiet. Doesn't take his eyes off me, and I don't raise mine.*)

I:

—Give me your address, in case...

—You don't know our address?

—No, Volodya always came to me and I've never written to him...

—You didn't know about *us*, father, mother, brothers?

—I knew he had family. And that he loved it.

—So, what kind of relationship is that . . . an inhuman one?
(*We're quiet*)
—That means—you never loved him—just as I thought—because no one leaves a beloved woman—or—a loving one . . .
—You can think whatever you like, but know one thing—and tell your parents: I've done nothing bad to him, not anything bad, ever.
—This is all strange, very strange. But however, he's—an actor, and you—a woman writer . . . *Please*, forgive me. I was abrupt, I wasn't in control of myself, I wasn't expecting this . . . I know that this isn't the way to talk to women. You were very kind to me. You could have simply thrown me out the door. But if you only knew what sort of sorrow there is—at home. What do you think—is he alive?
—He's alive.
—But why them isn't he writing? Even to you?
—He is—writing, and he has written to you many times—but the letters don't reach here.
—And you don't think that he has—perished?
—God forbid! No.
—This is what I'll tell my parents. That you're sure, that he's—thank God!—(*makes a wide cross*)—alive—and that he's writing—and that . . . And now I'll go. Do you forgive me?
—There wasn't any offence.
Already by the exit:
—How do you live—without a lock on the door? And at night you don't lock it? And how strange your flat is: dark, huge, and full of corridors . . . Will you allow me to visit you occasionally?
—I'd be heartily glad of it.
—Well, may God be with you!
—May God be—with *us*!

―――――

He never came back.

―――――

So, to finish about Yury Z. Right before my departure from Russia, in fact in April of 1922, in some sort of civil institution, where I went to get some papers, on a big wide stone staircase, I met him for the last time. He was going down, I was going up. A second's delay, a hesitation—I look and keep quiet—like back then, like always: looking upward, and again on—a staircase! His face looked—as if caught, as if as a whole he was—caught. He began to flutter like a big bird:

—You, you don't think, you didn't understand, you misunderstood... Everything is so complicated... so very not-simple...

—Yes, yes, of course, I know. I knew it long ago... Farewell, Yury Alexandrovich. Farewell forever. I'm leaving in a day or two, leaving—forever...

And I'm up the stairs, and he's down. And we're apart.

About the characters in this story, in a nutshell:

Pavlik A.—married, with two daughters (one of whom—maybe in Sonechka's memory, is a beauty), published.

Yury Z.—married, with a son, acting.

Verochka—his sister—whom I met in Paris afterward and about whom—a separate story, died from consumption in Yalta in 1930, a day before her death she wrote in pencil her last postcard to me:

"Marina! My heartsickness for you is as huge as this elephant."

They were brother and sister, and had one heart between them, and the whole of it went to the sister...

Volodya—went missing in the South in the same summer of 1919.

Irina—singing Hallidah—died in 1920, in a children's home.

Evgeny Bagartionovich Vakhtangov—died in Russia a long time ago.

Vakhtang Levanovich Mchedelov—died in Russia a long time ago.

Yura S. (who gave a little pie to Alya) died here, in Paris, after achieving fame.

About the other Yura—Yura N. (with whom we climbed to the rooftop)—I don't know anything.

Alya went to Moscow in 1937 and is an artist.

The house in Borisoglebsky is—still standing. Of my two elm trees, one is—still there.

I said: "characters." In essence there are no characters in my story. There is love. And it acted—through persons.

The more I bring you to life, the more I'm dying myself, dying of life—to you, into you—dying. The more you're—here, the more I'm—there. As if the barrier between the dead and the living were already removed, and both of these were moving freely back and forth in time and space—and into their opposite places. My death is—a fee for your life. In order for Hades' shadows to come alive, they need to drink living blood. But I went further than Odysseus,[114] I let you drink—mine.

April 29, 1922, Russian April—as I used to say and write in demotic. In an hour, I'm—leaving to go abroad. *That's that.*

A knock on the door. On the threshold—Pavlik A., whom I hadn't seen—for maybe a year.

His solemn eyes, already huge, widened with horror. With a corresponding voice (his voice was huge, strange—for such a small body), but this time: the hugest possible: with a voice of the whole of Hades' halls:

—I found out, E. Y. told me, that you are going abroad . . . today?

—Yes, Pavlik.

—Marina Ivanovna, may I come in?

—No. I've got only an hour—before departure. I must . . . collect my thoughts, say farewell to places . . .

—For one minute?

—It has already passed, Pavlik.

—But I'll still tell you, I must tell you (*deep gulp*)—Marina, I'm endlessly sorry about each minute of those years I spent *not* with you . . .

(My hair stood up. The words were from Sonechka's letter . . . That means she's with me now, with the lips of her poet—saying goodbye!)

—Pavlik, there's no time. But there is one thing: if you ever—at least a bit!—loved me, find my Sonechka Holliday for me.

He, in a voice, crushed with offence:

—I promise.

---

114 In Homer, *Odyssey* XI, Odysseus travels to the Underworld, where the shades of the dead gather, drink blood, and then talk to him.

Now—a long dash. A dash of three thousand versts[115] and seven years: two thousand five hundred and fifty-five days.

I'm on a walk with my two-year-old son in Park Bellevue, Observatoire. Next to me, on my other side, in step with my two-year-old son, walks Pavlik A., who came here with Vakhtangov's Studio. He has two daughters and (I think) a son.

—And . . . My Sonechka?

—Holliday is married and plays in the provinces.

—Happy?

—That I couldn't tell you.

And that's that.

One more dash—even longer: a whole ten years. Friday, May 14, 1937. Mur,[116] who was a two-year old and is now a twelve-year-old, and I walk down to our Metro station Mairie d'Issy, somewhere near the shop *Provence*. He said—to me, to be exact—to himself:

—The American *Sundey*[117] is the same as a *Dimanche Illustré*![118]—And what does that mean, "Holiday"? A free day, in general—a vacation.

—It means—a celebration. That was the name of the woman whom I, out of all women in the world, loved the most. And maybe—more than anyone. I think—more than anything. Sonechka Holliday. If only you could have such wife, Mur!

He, indignantly:

—Ma-ma!

—I'm not saying *her*, she isn't young now, she's only three years younger than I.

—I don't want to marry an old woman! I don't want to marry at all.

---

115 An obsolete Russian unit of distance, equal to 0.6629 miles.
116 Mur, the pet name of Tsvetaeva's son, Georgy Efron.
117 As spelled in the original.
118 Sunday comics.

—Don't be a fool. I'm not saying: marry Sonechka Holliday, but someone like Sonechka. However—there isn't *anyone* like her, so you can calm down—and nobody at all is worthy of her.

—Mama! You see, I don't know her, you talk about someone *you* know—of course, you can tell me . . .

—But you aren't—interested . . .

He's thinking of the newspaper with the American Mickey Mouses waiting for him at the stand on the corner of Boulevard Raspail:

—No, I'm very interested . . .

—Mur, she was a little girl, and (*looking for words*)—a real little devil! She had two long, long dark braids . . .

Mur makes an involuntary grimace: *au temps des cheveux et des chevaux.*[119]

. . . and she was small . . . so much smaller than you (*his grimace grows*)—because you're already bigger than me . . . (*tempting him*) and she was so brave that: under fire she took dinner to the cadets at the Cathedral of Christ the Savior . . .

—But why were the cadets dining in the Cathedral?

—That's not important. What's important is the "under fire." I told her at our farewell: "Sonechka, whatever happens to me, while you *exist* everything is good." She was the most beautiful thing I'd ever seen in my life, the sweetest thing I'd ever eaten in my life . . . (Mur: "Ugh Mama!") She wrote letters to me, and in one of them, in her last letter, she wrote: "Marina! How much I love your hands, which should only be kissed, but they move cupboards and carry tons . . ."

—Well, that's just—romanticism! Why—kissed?

—Because . . . because . . . (*prenant l'offensive*[120])—and what do you have against that?

—Nothing, if she'd written (*hesitating, looking for words*) . . . which should only be smelling flowers . . .

Then, understanding, he first starts laughing shyly.

---

119 *Du temps des Cheveux et des Chevaux: Souvenirs du Second Empire* [From the time of hair and horses: souvenirs of the Second Empire] is by Gyp, the pseudonym of Comtesse de Martel de Janville (1850–1932). The thought is that Tsvetaeva appears to Mur to be talking about the distant past.

120 Taking the offensive.

—Yes, yes, Mur, each finger with two nostrils! How many nostrils all together, Mur?

We both laugh. I, go on:

—And she said one more thing to me: "Marina, to know that you exist is to know, that there is no death."

—Well, that's just *flatteur*.[121]

—Why do you think that? She simply said something that is so, something that was so, because the life force came from me—and would come now too, and does come . . . but nobody wants it!

—Yes, yes, of course, I understand, but still . . .

—I'll definitely write to Alya, to see if she can find her, because I need her to know that there's nobody, nobody during my whole life I felt this way about . . .

We're by the metro and the conversation ended.

A small dash—only one day: May 15, 1937, a Saturday. An airmail letter from Russia—a heavy one. I open it, and the first thing I see at the very end is "Sonechka Holliday," and I already know. And here is *what*—I already know:

"Mama! I forgot to write you! I found a trace of Sonechka Holliday, your Sonechka—but too late. She died last year from liver cancer—without suffering. She didn't know she was sick with cancer. She was one of the best readers in the provinces and only two years ago came back to Moscow. They say that she was incredibly, unbelievably talented . . ."

And here is—a second piece of news, already widespread: a story from a sister of one of Sonechka's girlfriends[122]—to Alya, who wrote it down and sent to me:

"She got married to the director of a provincial theater, who loved her very much and was very devoted to her. All those years—from 1924 to her death—Sonya spent in the provinces, but she visited Moscow pretty often. We were all trying to convince her to get a job and settle in Moscow, but somehow

---

121 Flattery.

122 The quote, with some minor changes, is from a letter to Alya from Elizaveta Pavlovna Redlich (1897–1988).

she couldn't. Of course, if Vakhtangov had been alive, Sonya's life would have been different. Her whole life would have gone differently. K-v[123] liked her a lot, he was generally a kind and soft-hearted person, but he couldn't help her. Besides, his family was very jealous and Sonya had a hard time being there. It was hard . . . She practically didn't see Z-sky. Seldom, very seldom. As for S.,[124] he was passionate about her for a while, about her gift, but passions don't last long.

She should have done dramatic readings, but she was so attached to the theater! She dissipated her energies. In the theater, of course—it's more difficult. In provincial theaters she was, well . . . like a diamond! But she rarely had good roles. If she'd done dramatic readings—alone on stage—can you imagine? Yes, she was a tiny—a tiny-little thing. She often played children. How much she loved the theater! If you only knew how she played—no, not only in the sense of playing a role (I rarely saw her, she mainly worked in the provinces)—but she was a real hero. A few years ago, the pain in her stomach became terrible. But she sat behind the curtain with a hot-water bottle, right there, then went on stage, played her part, and then, as soon as the curtain came down, back to the hot-water bottle.

—(*Alya:*) But how come, when the pain started, she didn't go to the doctor, or wasn't taken?

—She came to Moscow and went to a very good homeopath. He gave her medicine and the pains disappeared. Afterward, she went only to that homeopath. She lived this way for four years and always felt well. Last time, when she came to Moscow, I found that she was awfully thin, just eyes, and her whole face had become very small. She'd changed a lot, but she didn't know that; even when she looked in the mirror, she didn't see it. Then her husband told me that she couldn't eat anything. We called the doctor and he said that we would have to call a surgeon. The surgeon examined her carefully and asked if there was any cancer in her family. She said no. Then he told her that she has to go to the hospital. We, of course, hid what she had from her. She desperately didn't want to be in the hospital, she cried all the time and said: "This is the

---

123 Vasily Ivanovich Kachalov (1875–1948), one of Russia's most renowned actors, who worked closely with Konstantin Stanislavsky and led the Kachalov Group within the Moscow Art Theatre. There are some letters of Sonechka to him in the archives of the theater.

124 Stanislavsky.

way to a coffin! This is a coffin!" But in the hospital, she calmed down, cheered up and started making different plans. They operated on her. But when they opened her up, they saw that it was too late. The doctors said she had only a few days to live.

Her husband and my sister always visited her. She didn't know she was dying. All the time she talked about how she'd live and work in the future. My sister visited her on the day of her death and so did her husband and someone else. Sophia Evgenevna loved order and asked the nurse to tidy up her room (she was alone in the room). Many flowers were brought to her and the nurse put them in water and cleaned everything. Sonya said: "And now I'll go to sleep." She turned away, settled comfortably in her bed and fell asleep. She died in her sleep.

I don't remember the time or day of her death. I wasn't in Moscow. My sister, perhaps, remembers it. I think it was—close to dawn. When did it happen? In the summer, yes, in the summer. When the Chelyuskins[125] returned.

She so very often remembered your mama, so often told us about her and you, so often read her poems. No, she never ever forgot her.

... After her death her husband went somewhere, disappeared. Where he is now is unknown.

Sonya was burned.

"When the Chelyuskins returned . . ." That's means—in the summer of 1934. So, not a year ago, but a whole three years. But a year—or three—or three days—I won't see her anymore, which—I always knew—and she'll never know how much...

No! She always—knew.

"When the Chelyuskins returned . . ."—sounds almost like: "when the swallows returned" ... it sounds like a phenomenon of nature, or maybe even better, in its scope and simplicity, even in its common-people-way, an indefinite marking—of date and time.

After all, my beginning with her—had no precise date, but was "in the time of the first tiny green leaves . . ."

---

125 Soviet steamships, reinforced to navigate the ice-bound Arctic waters.

Yes, it burns me that Sonechka—was burned, that there isn't a cross—to write on—as she asked:

> And it ended with a refrain:
> —Oh, my little one!

But—I see her in the fire and *don't* see her—in the ground! She didn't have that submissiveness and patience at all, which is equally required by an outmoded body or a not-yet-living seed. There wasn't anything in her of seed, she was all there:

> Yes, I know—from where I came!
> Ever hungry like a flame,
> I consume myself and glow.
> Light grows all that I conceive,
> Ashes everything I leave:
> Flame I am assuredly.[126]

It burns, of course. So there won't be—if I ever returned—a place to come and stand. Nothing to stand above. Sonechka is not there—at all. There aren't even her little bones. But Sonechka—little bones...no!

> Infanta, know this: I'm ready to burn at any stake...

The first thing I heard about her was: fire, the last one: burned. The first that I heard about her was: fire, and the last one: fire.

How strangely, in the contrary way, Pavlik's lines came true:

> As long as I know your eyes will gaze on me...—

—After all, they burned—Infanta, while the Dwarf—watched: her, ever-young, burning, fireproof: him grey-haired, wised-up—that's Infanta's Dwarf!

---

126   *Ja! ich weiss woher ich stamme:*
       Unersättlich wie die Flamme
       Nähr ich und verzehr ich mich!
       Glut wird alles, was ich fasse,
       Kohle—alles, was ich lasse,—
       Flamme bin ich sicherlich!
       From Friedrich Nietzsche, *Ecce Homo: How One Becomes What One Is* (1908).

If it had been up to me—I'd have taken the ashes and scattered them from the top of that high mountain (I intended for myself)—to all the corners of the earth—to all the loved ones: the ones that never yet were loved and the future ones. Even from—Vorobevs' Hill (where I and Sonechka never got to go: I had—children, stood in lines... she had—love...)

But what if I am—doing *it*? *Doing*—it! Not from any mountain, not even from a hill: from the palm of Lacanau-Océan, I scatter her ashes—to all of you with love, for the ones that didn't yet have it and the ones that will!

And now—farewell, Sonechka!

"May you be blessed for that moment of blissful happiness which you gave to another lonely and grateful heart!

My God! A whole moment of happiness! Is that too little for the whole of a person's life?..."[127]

(Lacanau-Océan, Summer 1937)

---

127 Dostoevsky, *White Nights*.

Autobiography[1]

January, 1940, Golitsyno[2] (Soviet Union)

I was born on September 26th, 1892 in Moscow. My father was Ivan Vladimirovich Tsvetaev, professor at Moscow University, founder of and curator at the Museum of Fine Arts (now the Museum of Visual Arts), and a prominent philologist. My mother was Maria Alexandrovna Mein, a passionate musician, who passionately loved poems and wrote them herself. A passion for poetry came from my mother, a passion for work and nature, from both parents.

First languages: German and Russian, and, by the age of seven, French. Mother's reading aloud and music. Undine, Rostam and Sohrab,[3] and *A Woodland Queen*[4] were things I read myself, also Nello and Patrasche.[5] A favorite thing to do from the age of four was reading and, from five, writing. Everything that I love I came to love before seven, and after that I didn't come to love anything. Now as a forty-seven-year-old I can tell that all I was fated to learn I learned before seven, and all the following forty years were a bringing of it to consciousness.

My mother was herself a lyrical element. I'm the oldest daughter of my mother, but the beloved one I was not. She was proud of me, but she loved the second one. I had an early grudge due to that deficiency of love. Childhood

---

1   The text we have translated is that printed in A. Saakyants and L. Mnukhin, *Marina Tsvetaeva, Sobraniye Sochinyenei v Syeme Tomakh* Tom 5 (Moscow, 1994), 6–8.
2   A town in Odintsovsky District, Moscow.
3   The tragedy of Rostam and Sohrab forms part of the tenth-century Persian epic *Shahnameh* by the poet Ferdowsi.
4   By Claude Adhémar André Theuriet (1833–1907), a French poet and novelist.
5   *A Dog of Flanders* (1872), a novel by the English author Marie Louise Ramée, published under her pseudonym Ouida, about a Flemish boy Nello and his dog Patrasche.

before ten: the old house in Three Pond Lane (Moscow) and a lonely dacha, Pesochnaya on the Oka River, near the city of Tarusa in Kaluga province.

My first school was the music school of Zograph-Plaksina in Merzlyakov Lane, where I started as the youngest student, not yet fully six years-old. The next one was Gymnasium IV, where I started in the preparatory class. In the fall of 1902, I left with my sick mother for the Italian Riviera, the city of Nervi, not far from Genoa, where I for the first time encountered Russian revolutionaries and the concept of Revolution. I wrote revolutionary poems, which were published in Genoa. In the spring of 1902, I started as a student in a French boarding school in Lozanne,[6] where I stayed for a year and a half. I wrote poems in French. In the summer of 1904, I went to Germany with my mother, to the Black Forest, where in the fall I started in a boarding school in Freiburg. I wrote poems in German. My most favorite book of these years was *Lichtenstein* by W. Hauff.[7] In the summer of 1906, I returned with my mother to Russia. Mother, not making it to Moscow, died in the dacha, Pesochnaya, near the city of Tarusa.

In the fall of 1906, I started as a student at Von-Derviz boarding gymnasium for girls[8] in Moscow. I wrote revolutionary poems. After the Von-Derviz gymnasium came the Alferova's boarding school, after which I spent my VI and VII grades in Brukonenko School (as a day student). I spent summers abroad, in Paris and Dresden. Friendship with the poet Ellis[9] and the philologist Nilender.[10] In 1910, while still at school, I published my first book of poems, *The Evening Album*, with poems I wrote at fifteen, sixteen, seventeen, and I met the poet M. Voloshin,[11] who wrote the first big article about me (if I'm not mistaken). In the summer of 1911, I went to him in Koktebel[12] and

---

6   In eastern France.

7   An historical novel, published in 1826.

8   Tsvetaeva was expelled "for freethinking and impudence" in 1906, just six months after she entered it.

9   Lev Lvovich Kobylinsky (pseudonym Ellis) (1879–1947), a poet, translator, theorist of symbolism, Christian philosopher, and historian of literature. He was in love with Tsvetaeva.

10 Vladimir Ottovich Nilender (1883–1965), a Russian and Soviet translator, poet, and literary critic. He too was in love with Tsvetaeva.

11 Maximilian Alexandrovich Kirienko-Voloshin (1877–1932), commonly known as Max Voloshin, a Russian poet of Ukrainian-German origin.

12 Koktebel, one of the most popular resorts in South-Eastern Crimea.

there I met my future husband, Sergey Efron, who was seventeen and from whom I haven't parted ever since. I married him in 1912. In 1912, my second book of poems, *A Magic Lantern*, came out and my first daughter, Ariadna, was born. In 1913, my father died.

From 1912 to 1922, I wrote non-stop, but did not publish any books. I was published a few times, though, in the periodical magazine *Northern Notes*.[13]

From the beginning of the Revolution till 1922, I lived in Moscow. In 1920, my second daughter, Irina, died at three years old in a children's shelter. In 1922, I went abroad, where I stayed for 17 years, three-and-a-half of which I spent in Czechia and fourteen in France. In 1939, I returned to the Soviet Union, following my family, and in order to give my son Georgy (born in 1925) a homeland.

Of the writers, my favorite ones are: Selma Lagerlöf,[14] Sigrid Undset,[15] Mary Webb.[16]

From 1922 to 1928 the following books of mine appeared in print: from Gosinzdat[17] *The Tsar-Maiden*; in 1916 "Versts" and a collection titled *Versts*; in Berlin, from different publishing houses, the narrative poem *The Tsar-Maiden*, the books of poems *Separation*, *Poems to A. Blok*, *The Craft*, and *Psyche*, which is far from including everything written from 1912 to 1922.

In Prague in 1924, I published my narrative poem *Swain*. In Paris in 1928, a book of poems *After Russia*. I didn't publish any other separate books. In the periodical press abroad I had: lyric plays which were written in Moscow, *Fortuna*, *An Adventure*, *The End of Casanova*, *Snowstorm*; narrative poems: "The Poem of the Mountain," "The Poem of the End," "A Staircase," "From the Sea," "An Attempt at a Room," "A Poem of Air," two parts of the trilogy *Theseus*, Pt. I "Ariadna," Pt. II "Fedora," "New Year-ish," "The Red Steer," and "Siberia."

Translations into French: "*La Gars*" (a translation of my poem "Swain," unabridged), with illustrations by N. Goncharova, a translation of some of

---

13   A magazine published in St. Petersburg (1913–1917).
14   Selma Ottilia Lovisa Lagerlöf (1858–1940), a Swedish author, teacher, and the first female writer to win the Nobel Prize in Literature.
15   Sigrid Undset (1882–1949), a Norwegian novelist, awarded the Nobel Prize for Literature in 1928.
16   Mary Gladys Webb (1881–1927), an English romantic novelist and poet.
17   State Publishing House, founded in 1919.

Pushkin's poems, a translation of Russian and German revolutionary songs, and of Soviet songs too. After my return to Moscow, I translated some poems by M. Lermontov. I didn't have any more of my translations published.

Prose: "The Hero of Labor" (meeting with V. Bryusov[18]), "A Living Word About a Living Man" (meeting with M. Voloshin), "A Captive Spirit" (meeting with A. Bely[19]), "Natalia Goncharova"[20] (life and works). Tales from my childhood: "The House Near Old Pimen," "Mother and Music," "A Devil," and so on. Articles: "Art in the Light of Conscience," "Two Forest Kings." Short stories: "Chlustovki," "The Opening of the Museum," "The Ivy Tower," "The Intended," "The Chinese Man," "Mother's Fairytale," and many others. Everything in my prose is autobiography.

---

18 Valery Yakovlevich Bryusov (1873–1924), a Russian poet, prose writer, dramatist, translator, critic, and historian.

19 Andrey Bely (1880–1934), a Russian poet, novelist, short story writer, autobiographer, essayist, and critic.

20 Natalia Sergeevna Goncharova (1881–1962), a Russian avant-garde artist, painter, costume designer, writer, illustrator, and set designer.

www.ingramcontent.com/pod-product-compliance
Lightning Source LLC
Chambersburg PA
CBHW031423160426
43196CB00008B/1024